THE ART OF
KIKI's
DELIVERY SERVICE

THE ART OF
KIKI's
DELIVERY SERVICE

The Hopes and Hearts of Today's Girls

Screenplay written, directed and produced by Hayao Miyazaki

———————————— ✦✦✦✦✦✦ ————————————

The wonderful children's book *Kiki's Delivery Service* (written by Eiko Kadono and published by Fukuinkan Shoten publishers in Japan) gives an affectionate depiction of the hopes and spirit of today's girls struggling to become independent. In previous tales, spiritual independence comes with the protagonist's economic independence. Now, as the recent expressions, freelance part-time worker, slacker, and *torabayu* (editor's note: changing jobs) indicate, economic independence doesn't necessarily include spiritual independence. Nowadays spiritual poverty is a much more urgent matter than material poverty.

Leaving home can't really be considered a rite of passage these days. You only need a nearby convenience store to live in a world of strangers. The issues of independence girls have to confront now are in some ways more difficult since they must discover, develop, and then actualize their talents.

There are girls, for example, who move to Tokyo hoping to pursue a career in the manga industry. According to surveys, there are 300,000 kids who'd like to become manga artists. Given how common the profession is now, it's pretty easy to be published. One can even make a living at it. The real challenge occurs when it becomes a routine part of your life. While her mother's broom might give Kiki protection, her father's radio solace, and her black cat a friendly sidekick, Kiki experiences loneliness—a yearning to connect with others. She represents every girl who is drawn to the glamour of the big city but find themselves struggling with their newfound independence—in spite of their parents' love and financial support. Today's girls also share Kiki's naiveté and lack of awareness.

In the original story, Kiki resolves each dilemma she encounters with resolve, and in doing so, she develops a circle of friends. For the anime, we had to alter this premise slightly. Although it is nice to see her talent bloom so gracefully, today's city girls are much weaker and jaded in spirit. For many girls, the struggle to achieve independence is too demanding. Many of them feel like they're treading water. We wanted to explore this issue of independence more thoroughly in the filmed version. As a result, the film has a realistic edge. The isolation and disillusionment Kiki experiences are much stronger in the film than they are in the original story.

When I first came across Kiki, the first image that occurred to me was a small girl flying across the city at night. A sea of lights—but not a single one offers her a warm welcome. There's a profound loneliness high above the city. In flying, one may no longer be confined to land, but this freedom also implies insecurity and loneliness. The heroine of our film is a girl who defines herself by flying. There have been many animation films based on "witch girls," but their magic is only a device to realize their wishes. They function as celebrity idols without any real problems. The witch's magic in *Kiki's Delivery Service* doesn't come so easily.

Magic in this film is a limited power no different from the talents of any average girl.

Later on, as she flies above the city, Kiki feels a strong connection to the people below, but her sense of self is much stronger than it was at the beginning. We realize that our film's story must develop in a convincing manner in order to make the film end on this happy note.

We have no desire to dismiss the flamboyance of young girls. We only wish our viewers won't be too spellbound by the flamboyance of youth. Ultimately, this film celebrates their struggle to become independent (After all, we were all boys and girls at one time; the struggle is just as urgent for our younger staff). We also believe this is absolutely essential for the film to succeed as a work of entertainment for its message must be relevant and universal.

HAYAO MIYAZAKI

P. 1   Kiki and Jiji/concept sketch. (Katsuya Kondo)
P. 2   Illustration for theater posters.
P. 4   Cover for February 1989 issue of monthly magazine, *Animage*.
       (cel drawing/Hayao Miyazaki   background/Kazuo Oga)

PART ONE
IN THE
BEGINNING

Kiki's Delivery Service originated in Studio Ghibli in Kichijoji, Tokyo.

Kiki's Delivery Service was Miyazaki's follow-up to the multi-award winning film, *My Neighbor Totoro*. It was Studio Ghibli's fourth theatrical release feature film. For Miyazaki, whose films were based on his original stories, *Kiki's Delivery Service* was the first non-original story he worked on since *Meitantei Holmes*. His dedication to the film was nothing short of extraordinary, given how he not only directed, but also produced and wrote the screenplay. Initially Miyazaki wasn't supposed to be involved with *Kiki's Delivery Service* at all. He ended up producing, writing and directing the film because of various circumstances.

The film production company Fudosha first brought the project to Tokuma Publishers, with a proposal to turn Eiko Kadono's original story into a film directed by either Hayao Miyazaki or Isao Takahata.

The project began in the spring of 1987 when the production for *My Neighbor Totoro* became official. Because it would have been impossible for Miyazaki or Takahata to direct the project while working on *My Neighbor Totoro* and *Grave of the Fireflies*, Miyazaki was assigned to produce this film—which would now be directed by a young talented director.

Miyazaki based his film concept on the resemblance he saw between the heroine of *Kiki's Delivery Service* and the young women animators at the studio. They all shared the dilemmas young women experienced in the city. Given how the character Kiki was an average girl, the film could only be 70-80 minutes long. At first, *Kiki's Delivery Service* was only intended to be a small-scale theatrical release with a running time not to exceed 80 minutes.

Various staff members were selected between the end of 1987, when *My Neighbor Totoro* approached completion, and the spring of 1988. Katsuya Kondo, who participated in the production of *Castle in the Sky* and *My Neighbor Totoro*, was brought in for key animation and character design, Shinji Otsuka for key animation. Kazuo Oga from *My Neighbor Totoro* recommended Hiroshi Ono who had worked on *Samia Don, Cat's Eye,* and *Akira* for art direction.

The most critical issue of course was finding the director and screenwriter. A young animation screenwriter was hired, but selecting a director proved to be difficult. In the midst of his hectic schedule for *My Neighbor Totoro*, Miyazaki had screened numerous animation videos by young animation directors, but he couldn't find anyone appropriate. Furthermore, Miyazaki wasn't happy with the draft written by the young screenwriter. The approach was interesting, but it departed too much from Miyazaki's approach. He found the screenwriter's approach too cold. This screenplay was subsequently shelved.

(Continued on page 11)

Kiki's Delivery Service, The Original Story

The original story *Kiki's Delivery Service* was published as part of the Fukuinkan Children's Books series in 1985. It was awarded the Hans Christian Anderson Award in Japan, the Noma Children's Literature Award, and the Shogakukan Literature Award. Reprinted several times, the story remains popular today.

Each sequence in the story tends to be resolved perhaps because it was serialized in the magazine *Haha no Tomo* (Mother's Friend) (and subsequently modified for the book edition). The book resembles the film up until Kiki's departure for the city, but once she begins her delivery service, the plot mostly revolves around her efforts to make difficult deliveries. The story develops as she becomes acquainted with the city and matures with each little episode. She is taken in by the city's inhabitants not as a result of the airship incident (which only occurs in the film), but because she manages to rescue a child snatched by the sea at the beach.

The film adapts various episodes and characters in the first half of the original story, but the depiction of characters in the film varies from the book. Ursula is an anonymous "painter" and client in the original story. Also, Tombo (in the original he is "Tombo-san") ends up befriending and assisting her as a result of breaking her broom. Kiki only become conscious of Tombo-san when she must deliver a girl's love letter. This sequence is elaborately described, but their personalities seem a little immature compared to the characters in the film.

The film only covers a single summer, ending with Kiki's letter, but the original story takes place over a year, the final chapter describing her visit home after her training is completed. Although her intention was to stay home for a while, upon returning she realizes how much she misses Corico. She cuts her stay short and flies back to the city. The story ends with her pointing down at Corico and declaring, "See, that's our city."

The original story was published in the Fukuinkan Children's Book series.

The illustrations in the book are pen drawings with a soft touch. Kiki has long hair and her physique convey more feminine tenderness. Most of the drawings are back views as if to spark the reader's imagination. The bird's-eye-view of her home village and Corico presented at the beginning and the end are exquisite. This might have to do with the artist's experience in map illustration.

The film had a pseudo-European setting, but the setting in the original is stranger, one that's neither western nor Japanese.

Other differences in the original story include Jiji not having a girlfriend, and Jiji being able talk to Kiki to the very end. The husband baker also says something besides, "hey."

Although it's not explained in the film, the bells hanging from the treetops in Kiki's home village were put there by her mother, Kokiri. She was hoping these bells would help Kiki concentrate while flying on her broom.

Eiko Kadono, the author of *Kiki's Delivery Service*, was born in Tokyo in 1935. After receiving her Bachelor of Arts in English at Waseda University, she worked in publishing and then moved to Brazil for two years. Upon her return, she began writing illustration books and fairy stories. She won the *Robou no Ishi* (Wayside Rock) Award in 1984. Her works include *Zubon Sencho-san no Hanashi* (Fukuinkan Shoten Publishers / winner of the Obunsha children's literature prize), and *Oodrobou-shi Burabura* (Kodansha / Sankei Children's Literature Prize in Culture).

Akiko Hayashi was born in Tokyo in 1945. She received her bachelor of arts from Yokohama National University in art. She worked as an illustrator for magazines and map publications, but with the publication of *Kamihikouki* (Fukuinkan Shoten Publishers / written by Minoru Kobayashi), she established herself as a children's book illustrator. Her extensive work includes *Hajimete no Otsukai* (Fukuinkan Shoten Publishers / written by Yoriko Tsutsui) and *Byunbyun Goma ga Mawattara* (Doshinsha / written by Hiro Miyakawa).

This logo for the film version of *Kiki's Delivery Service* was based on Akiko Hayashi's illustrations from the original story.

Corico is based on a city on the Swedish island of Gotland called Visby.

The setting for *Kiki's Delivery Service* is similar to Stockholm. In fact, the film's backstreets are based on the downtown district of Stockholm known as Gamla Stan.

(Continued from page 8)

My Neighbor Totoro was completed in April, 1988. No longer pressed for time, Miyazaki began working on the screenplay for *Kiki's Delivery Service* in spite of his intended role as producer. Because the film would have a European look, he proposed a research trip for the main staff. They would visit the first foreign country he ever visited, Sweden, and its Gotland Island.

The key animators Shinji Otsuka and Katsuya Kondo, art director Hiroshi Ono, and assistant director Sunao Katabuchi joined Miyazaki. They visited Visby, a city on the Swedish island of Gotland. They photographed landscapes of streets and buildings, ending up with 80 rolls of 24-exposure film and three boxes of research material.

After their return to Japan, they began work on the concept art. As Miyazaki sent his screenplay in weekly installments, they also began work on character designs and concept sketches.

As he worked on the screenplay Miyazaki's ideas rapidly expanded. The painter who appears as a client in the original story became Ursula. He also came up with the climactic scene for the airship panic scene. The draft of the screenplay was completed on June 18 and the revised version was finalized on July 8. Although the screenplay was based on the original story, the film now had Miyazaki's imprint. He now had no other choice but to direct the film as well.

After finishing the screenplay he began storyboarding, but as it will become apparent later, because he wanted to take a new approach to directing *Kiki's Delivery Service*, the process became unexpectedly time consuming. Only Part A was completed by the end of August. Color design supervisor Michiyo Yasuda joined the initial staff in July in conjunction with the selection of the staff for key animation, in-between/clean-up animation, ink and paint, and background art.

Once Miyazaki became the director of this film the initial running time was extended from 80 minutes to 90 minutes, but as the storyboarding progressed and various parts expanded (the sequence with the old dog Jefferson significantly altered the screenplay), it became a major film with a total running time of 102 minutes.

Miyazaki offers his views on filmmaking:

"When I make a film, I begin by having a very clear concept of why I have to make it in the first place. What kind of film will it be? What is going to be conveyed? What is our purpose in making this film? Will the audience accept it? These are the issues I confront, but I don't make films to send out a message. That might be part of the work involved in clarifying the concept, but it's not enough to send a message. The film has to be entertaining."

Miyazaki's statement could be considered a message to Japan's film industry, including the world of animation.

お姉さん 急いで!!

These concept sketches were based on the original story, but never used for the film. Katsuya Kondo, Shinji Otsuka, Yoshifumi Kondo, and Sunao Katabuchi produced countless drawings before Miyazaki became the director of the film.

Kiki (black dress)

くろ服 BL (ス)
しろ服]100
ハイライト] 90
画 W 90

R40 / AR20
21 / R-11
OP-1 T·P / OP-2 T·P
H·B / EK45
VG-4 / VG-5

R40 / AR20
H·B / EK45
21 / R-11
OP-1 / OP-2 T·P
アツミ BL
YR80M / OH-1
かご PH-9
PH-8 / PH-7 ボタン
VG-4 / VG-5
ORH-6 / ORH-7
かち VG-6
あ-8 / KH-8
R-17 / FH-8
ORH-10 / ORH-12
クツのそこ YR-B

Part of the color assignment book assigned to the ink and paint staff. The color design for each part of the character is assigned in detail to achieve color consistency for the cels. The color numbers aren't unified because Ghibli uses a variety of paint subcontractors. Organizing this series is no easy task for the color design staff. There were 465 colors for *Kiki's Delivery Service*. TV animation only requires 200 colors. Consequently, *Kiki's Delivery Service* required more than twice the usual amount. Twenty-five of these colors were newly developed for the movie.

Miyazaki took a new approach in directing *Kiki's Delivery Service*. Previously, his production staff developed new processes such as the rubber multi-plane for the Ohmu's movement in *Nausicaä of the Valley of the Wind* or the lighting effects to depict the passage of time in *My Neighbor Totoro*, but *Kiki's Delivery Service* required an entirely new overall method.

Miyazaki took a new approach in the shot angles for *Kiki's Delivery Service*. For example, for dialogue scenes, instead of employing the usual close-up shots, he opted for eye-line shots approximating the characters' height. In terms of cityscape sequences, unlike previous films, there would be no panoramic shots of Tombo's house, only partial illustrations of the backside and front lawn that implied the overall image. For Kiki's small mezzanine kitchen, to illustrate the space in the past we would have included a scene depicting her ascending the narrow stairs, but this time we omitted this type of explicatory scenes.

Color assignment involves the selection of colors painted on the cels. Given how everything from props to the entire stage—as well as the characters—determine the colors painted on each cel, color assignment is a unique task, analogous to live action cinematography in terms of determining the film's look, but also involving the kind of color coordination required for costumes and stage design in live action films.

Originally, the art director also supervised color assignment (in the tradition of live action films), but once subcontracting work became common in the animation industry, color assignment became specialized in order to standardize colors. Of course, the art director and color assignment supervisor still had to collaborate, but in Miyazaki's films color assignment plays a significant role in determining the film's look.

Miyazaki offers his view on animation colors. "The reason animation films suffer creatively has to do with the fact that they all use the same colors. It's like 'oh, the color of animation.' Limiting color only narrows the animation film's potential. Color is absolutely critical for the film's look in *Kiki's Delivery Service*. The approach to color is very focused and concise. Lately, I've been reducing the colors significantly in the most crucial scenes. For example, action scenes without garish colors are very engaging.

(Continued on page 17)

Normal color assignment image. The contrast is extreme compared to the film's cel.

Same image with Studio Ghibli's color assignment. The restrained, soft color makes it warmer.

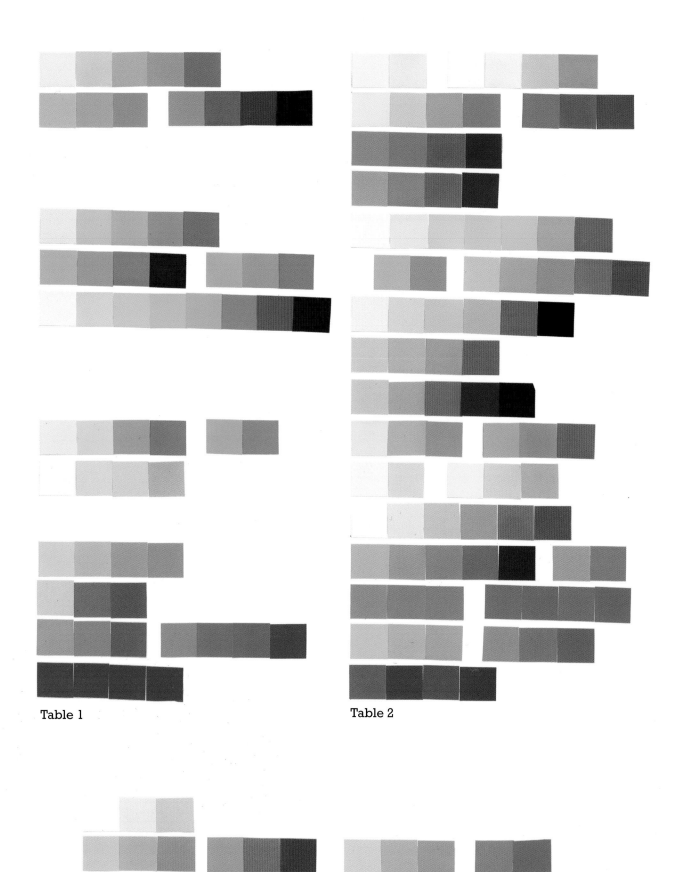

Table 1

Table 2

Table 3

(Continued from page 14)

"Other filmmakers have taken this approach, but I believe that Ghibli is the only studio that has really managed to develop such unique colors. If other studios end up being influenced and our colors become standard practice, that might transform the industry."

The veteran staff member of Ghibli, Michiyo Yasuda, supervised the color assignment. The recent change in her title to "color design" for this film further indicates how important this task is.

The following text was taken from Yasuda's color assignment description for Ghibli.

Normally we determine the colors for each character by following the director's overall concept for the film. By trial and error we apply provocative colors or matching colors and select the film's cel colors.

First, we will consider the shades of essential paints by examining the color samples (p. 16) used in films since *My Neighbor Totoro* (for now we'll leave aside the overall effectiveness of these colors).

I divided the color charts (color samples) into three groups. The charts are incomplete. They don't include brown, blue and gray colors.

Chart 1: Approximation of primary colors (overall they are bright. The most popular colors for most animation films).

Chart 2: Relatively natural colors (they have texture, but the colors are more restrained than the neutral colors used in animation films).

Chart 3: Nearly natural colors (the color is quite restrained).

When I say "restrained colors" in chart two and chart three, I don't mean murky or dirty colors. Of course, if you use murky colors, the image will end up murky. "Restraining" creates a transparent texture that will in fact enhance the image.

There are colors in charts two and three that would seem exceedingly dull on their own, but they can end up vivid and beautiful in backgrounds or in combination with other colors.

The colors in *Nausicaä of the Valley of the Wind* were restrained compared to previous films, but in order to increase the characters' luminosity, we decided to reduce the saturation. For *My Neighbor Totoro* and *Grave of the Fireflies* we came up with a light brown carbon that has a

softness that didn't go well with the colors from chart one so we needed a new color configuration.

◆*My Neighbor Totoro*

We used colors that were bright, cheerful as well as warm and inviting (this also meant that our colors were becoming less artificial, approaching natural textures). So we used the neutral colors of chart one and the natural colors in chart two. While the colors were saturated for the exterior green, the interior saturation was significantly reduced, so the most natural colors from chart three were used for the interior color combinations.

As the film proceeded into parts C and D, the restrained, natural colors of chart two were used instead of the colors from part A. As time gradually passes in part D, the colors in the art don't change, although the drawings manage to depict this shift. But for Satsuki's skin and her clothes we used restrained, soft colors.

◆*Grave of the Fireflies*

During pre-production we developed some of the colors for chart two and the most natural colors from chart three. These colors were developed in collaboration with the main staff—which included director Isao Takahata and animation supervising animator Yoshifumi Kondo. We developed them after the grueling process of testing many colors (approximately 250). (We relied on sources including the technical book, *Japan's Color*, a collection of natural colors that include *nibi*, *hi*, and *kurenai*, all colors taken from flowers, grass, trees, and ash.)

Almost 80 percent of the colors for *Grave of the Fireflies* came from the natural, restrained colors of chart three. The color saturation in the art as a result was also reduced. The colors in chart three might be hard to distinguish at a glance, and because they alter the texture somewhat, they might seem unnecessary, but they are very effective in 1) enhancing extremely light blues, 2) yellows, and 3) reds. As a result of reducing the saturation, these natural colors were depicted in the projected film (of course, this was thanks to the film processing supervisor).

For *Grave of the Fireflies* we created paints and applied them to the characters according to the director's concept of the film. The color assignment for each shot was based on this process. Each character's shading looks natural largely because we applied the proper shadow colors.

We based our color assignments for *Kiki's Delivery Service* on these colors we tested and developed for *My Neighbor Totoro* and *Grave of the Fireflies*.

◆*Kiki's Delivery Service*

When I first went over the character designs, I thought the colors should be somewhat flashy, but once I tried this, they only made the image look cheap and superficial. Given how our colors evolved in the two previous films toward a natural look, this also seemed like a regression. Because the protagonist is a girl, and the city is the main setting, we were better off avoiding primary colors, mainly applying the relatively natural looking ones from color chart two in conjunction with the neutral colors in chart one and the textures of chart three. Of course we used primary colors for details.

The skin color is even more restrained compared to *My Neighbor Totoro*, but also more textured compared to *Grave of the Fireflies* to enhance a "soft" look.

Hiroshi Ono's art had an overall soft look to it, but there would be parts where the saturation was extreme in either direction. We managed to preserve the feel of the image by applying natural textures instead of matching the saturation in the art. For example, when Kokiri prepares her potion, the drawing of flowers and plants is detailed, combining the high saturation of green along with low saturation colors, but the cel art came from charts two and three. The orange for Dora's clothes and the color of the medicine might seem dull on their own, but they are quite sufficient when seen on film. For the night scenes and the rain scenes, instead of matching the cel color to the background's darkness, we applied bright colors with restrained textures to accommodate the background art. Of course, the cel art will only work in conjunction with the countless, painstakingly detailed background drawings of the stone pavement, cityscapes, and interiors.

In their artistic quest, Hayao Miyazaki and Isao Takahata demand the closest attention to precise color design. Therefore, our work involves developing new colors, trying them out with each shot, each new film. Even Studio Ghibli hasn't come up with a defined color scheme because it's always evolving according to the approaches and requirements of each new film.

For *Nausicaä of the Valley of the Wind* the luminosity was increased and the colors were bright.

Earthy colors were used for *Castle in the Sky* to match the art.

With the application of brown carbon, the softness in the art could be conveyed. For *Kiki's Delivery Service*, carbon was applied for Kiki's village in order to make it look warmer than the noisy city. Conversely, normal carbon is used for the city with its bustling scenes including car traffic.

Natural colors were extensively tested for *Grave of the Fireflies* during pre-production.

© Akiyuki Nozaka, Shinchosha/Hakuhodo

The color situation is reduced to match the background of natural colors. The brown carbon trace lines were also highly effective.

PART TWO
ART OF
ANIMATED FILM

This collection of concept sketches, concept art, character designs, cel and film images follows the sequence of the story. The concept sketches are by Katsuya Kondo, Shinji Otsuka, and Yoshifumi Kondo. Concept art images are by Hiroshi Ono and character designs are by Katsuya Kondo. The commentary was based on interviews conducted with each artist.

Unprocessed cel images included in this collection may vary from the film's images.

1   Kiki stands up on the grassy knoll.
2   View of the village. (concept sketch by Yoshifumi Kondo)
3-4 Kiki lying on the grassy knoll. (concept sketch by Yoshifumi Kondo)

1

2

3

4

1

2

1 Hedge between pastures. (concept art)
2 Kiki hopping over the hedge. (film)
3 Tree-lined road. (concept art)
4 The fence above the hill. (concept art)

"By the time I drew these, the storyboards were completed so my layout was based on them. I paid attention to the scale and dimension of the trees. The color shading is affected by the processing for transmitted light and water surface, so the actual art must have been difficult for Kazuo Oga." (Hiroshi Ono)

3

4

1-3   Kiki. (character design)
4   Kiki in her domestic clothes. (rough sketch by Hayao Miyazaki)
5-7   Kiki. (concept sketch)

"Instead of making other people happy, Kiki is the kind of
person who ends up relying on others without realizing it.
What concerns her the most are her feelings and her happiness.
I didn't provide any instructions for the voice actor Minami
Takayama, but her performance was astonishingly good. She
claimed she could relate to Kiki's feelings." (Hayao Miyazaki)

4

5

6

7

1

2

3

4

5

6

7

8

1-2   Early version of Kiki with long hair.
3-4   Early version of Kiki as a well-off girl.
5-6   Early version of Kiki with long hair.
7   Different version with long hair.
8   Early version of Kiki with Jiji.
9-16   Early version of Kiki with bundled hair.

"Initially, I followed the original
story illustrations and drew Kiki
with long hair, but this would
have been difficult in terms
of animation. Still wanting
to be faithful to the original
story, I had her hair bundled
with ribbons to be removed
when she was alone in order
to convey her dual nature.
But this didn't really fit with
her character so she ended up
having short hair. I wanted her
cheeks to be reddish from the
start." (Katsuya Kondo)

9

10

11

12

13

14

こんなことは しません！

15

16

1

2

3

1   The Okino residence. (background)
2   The Okino residence. (concept art)
3   The Okino residence. (concept art by Katsuya Kondo)

"I wanted to emulate the original story's image of
Kiki's house being surrounded by flowers, giving it
a fairy tale look." (Hiroshi Ono)

1

2

3

4

5

1   The Okino residence. (cel art)
2   Kiki pokes her head into the sun room. (cel art)
3   Kiki runs into the sun room. (cel art)
4   View of sun room. (concept art)
5   Kiki tugs her hem to curtsey. (cel art)

"I wanted the interior and exterior of the sun room
to look bright, but I ended up having to reduce the
light quite a bit. This turned out to be better though."
(Hiroshi Ono)

1

2

1   Kokiri preparing her potion. (concept sketch by Yoshifumi Kondo)
2   Kokiri prepares her potion. (cel art)
3-4   Potion preparation sequence. (concept sketches by Shinji Otsuka)

"Kokiri ends up becoming a fellow citizen. She has her own set of
values to help her lead a peaceful life. She wants to be part of the
petit-bourgeois. She values being considerate toward others and
having a purpose in life. That's why she's dedicated to preparing
potions for the elderly." (Hayao Miyazaki)

3

4

39

1

2

1-2   Kokiri. (character designs)
3-5   Kokiri with wavy hair. (concept sketches)
4   Kokiri. (concept sketch)

3

4

5

1

2

1   Dora in the sun room. (cel art)
2   Dora. (character design)
3   Dora. (character alterations)

3

5

4

6

7

1

2

3

1   Jiji. (character designs)
2   Kiki and Jiji. (cel art)
3-5   Jiji. (concept sketches)
6   Kiki and Jiji. (concept art)

"After hearing Jiji's voice, I realized how odd he appears when he's assertive. It's because he's not very independent. He's part of Kiki. He represents an immature part of her." (Hayao Miyazaki)

1

1 Kiki in plain clothes. (concept sketch)
2 Kiki has Kokiri tie her ribbon.
(concept sketch by Yoshifumi Kondo)
3-5 Kiki puts on her black outfit. (cel art)

"Kiki acts like a child in front of her parents, but
when she's alone she has serious thoughts. While
she might be blunt toward boys her age, she's
respectful toward her seniors—particularly if she
admires them. She's not, however, a calculating
little girl. Her reactions—whether spontaneous, or
simply manners she acquired from her parents—
show how dynamic she is." (Hayao Miyazaki)

5

2

3

4

1-3 Kiki and her father Okino. (concept art by Yoshifumi Kondo)

4-6 Kiki and her father bonding. (cel art)

"In a conventional animation film, a dialogue scene would proceed with close-up shots, but this time, instead of employing this animation approach, we used a normal height perspective for our shot angles. Of course, that would lead to mismatched perspectives. That's why the balance is off and the size of the house is completely inconsistent [laughs]." (Hayao Miyazaki)

1

2

3

4

6

5

1

2

1   Kiki's father Okino. (character design)
2   Okino and Kokiri. (character design)
3-7 Okino. (character alterations)

"Kiki's father has no defining features so
he was difficult to draw. I ended up having
a hard time depicting him. I had the actors
Akira Terao and David McCallum in mind
while I was drawing." (Katsuya Kondo)

3

5

4

6

7

1

1   The moonlit Okino residence. (background)
2   Kiki and her classmates. (cel art)
3   Kiki and her classmates. (concept sketch)

2

3

1

2

1   Kokiri forces Kiki to take her broom. (cel art)
2   The night of her departure. (concept art by Shinji Otsuka)
3   Kiki in her black dress. (character design)
4   Kiki preparing to leave. (concept sketch)
5   Kiki preparing to leave. (concept sketch)
6   Kiki's bag. (concept sketch)

"Black dresses are pretty shabby looking, so having to
wear one while descending upon a crowd must be a
trying experience. Once she realizes the point to this
endeavor she'll start to comprehend the purpose of
her training." (Hayao Miyazaki)

3

4

5

あまり大くならないように・・・

キキのバック

6

1   Kiki concentrates and floats upward. (cel art)
2   The girls cheering for Kiki's journey. (cel art)
3   Kiki flies up into the stars toward the moon. (cel art)
4   Main Titles. (film)

"Because Kiki's flight is supposed to be unstable we didn't
do much repetitive animation here. I concentrated on her
walking rather than her flying movements. For example,
I wanted her skirt to flap around so it wouldn't look
eloquent." (Hayao Miyazaki)

3

1

2

魔女の宅急便

4

1

2

3

1-2   Kiki's flying style. (character designs)
3-4   Flying variations. (character designs)
5-7   Kiki's flying style. (concept sketches)
8   Flying variations. (character designs)

5

6

7

8

1

1 Kiki flying under a sea of stars. (cel art)
2 An enormous passenger airplane flies over Kiki in the sky. (film)
3 Kiki rides along without hands. (cel art)

"Because this was a girl's film I thought we should have a song here.
I had intended on using songs by Yumin (Yumi Matsutoya) from the
start. I first heard 'Message of Rouge' when I was still working at Nippon
Animation and I thought it was a good song back then. It doesn't
sound dated. In fact, I thought it would sound fresh to our audience
now. 'Message of Rouge' revolves around a girl's feelings. It isn't one
of those songs where the girl is pining for some guy's attention. Still, I
was amazed at how well it worked when I first saw it with the titles. We
thought of using 'Central Freeway,' but we couldn't really use it because
the lyrics contained proper nouns." (Hayao Miyazaki)

2

3

1

2

1   Senior witch. (character design)
2   Senior witch and her black cat. (cel art)
3   Senior witch. (concept sketch)
4   Senior witch waves to Kiki and descends. (cel art)
5   Senior witch's black cat. (character design)
6   Senior witch when she was referred to as "the sister witch." (concept sketch)

先輩魔女さん.

3

5

4

お姉さん魔女

6

63

1

2

3

1   Kiki flying through the thunderstorm. (cel art)
2   Kiki finds shelter in the freight train. (cel art)
3   Kiki takes off her drenched clothes. (cel art)
4   Hopeful Kiki and reluctant Jiji. (cel art)
5   Kiki flying next to the seagulls.

4

5

1

2

3

1   The city of Corico. (concept art)
2   Panoramic view of the square. (concept art)
3   Main street descending from the square. (concept art)

"This is how the Japanese imagine an old European city.
There are elements of Naples, Lisbon, Stockholm, Paris, and
San Francisco, all mixed in, so one side faces the Mediterranean
while the other faces the Baltic Sea [*laughs*]." (Hayao Miyazaki)

1

2

1 Kiki is drawn to Corico. (cel art)
2 Kiki approaching the clock tower. (concept art by Yoshifumi Kondo)
3 The old, clock tower keeper. (character design)
4 The old, clock tower keeper. (cel art)
5 The old, clock tower keeper. (concept sketch)

One idea was to have Kiki spend a night at the clock tower and befriend the old clock tower keeper. The illustration on page 20 is based on this concept.

4

3

5

1

2

3

4

5

6

7

1

2

3

1　Kiki flying through the shopping district.
　　(concept art by Shinji Otsuka)
2　Kiki makes a slow descent. (concept art by Yoshifumi Kondo)
3　Kiki flying through the shopping district. (concept art by
　　Yoshifumi Kondo)
4　Kiki lands on the street. (concept art by Yoshifumi Kondo)
5　Tombo sees Kiki. (concept art by Yoshifumi Kondo)
6　A policeman scolds Kiki. (concept art by Yoshifumi Kondo)
7　Kiki introduces herself wearing her best smile. (cel art)

"I didn't want this to turn into one of those 'celebrity
witch' films just because she has witch powers. At first she
attracts attention in the city but her flying ability turns out
to be no big deal for the inhabitants. I really worked on
making this premise convincing." (Hayao Miyazaki)

4

5

6

7

1

2

1-2 Tombo calls on the disappointed Kiki.
(concept art by Yoshifumi Kondo)
3 Tombo chases after Kiki.
(concept art by Katsuya Kondo)
4 Tombo chases after Kiki.
(concept art by Shinji Otsuka)
5 Tombo excited by Kiki's flying.
(concept art by Yoshifumi Kondo)
6 Kiki takes off, spurning Tombo.
(concept art by Katsuya Kondo)

3

4

5

6

1

2

1-2   Tombo. (character design)
3-4   Tombo. (concept sketches)
5-6   Tombo in fashionable clothes. (character designs)
7   Tombo. (character design)

"We already had a clear concept for Tombo, so drawing him was only a matter of execution. His hairstyle resembles the kind you see in foreign films. It seemed to work for Tombo." (Katsuya Kondo)

3

とんぼ

4

トンボ

5

6

7

1   Kiki wandering through the city.
    (concept sketch by Yoshifumi Kondo)
2   Kiki looking for a hotel.
    (concept sketch by Katsuya Kondo)
3   Kiki inside the hotel.
    (concept sketch by Shinji Otsuka)
4   Kiki at the hotel.
    (concept sketch by Shinji Otsuka)
5   Kiki sits under the park statue.
    (concept sketch by Shinji Otsuka)
6-7 Kiki passing by the bakery.
    (concept sketch by Katsuya Kondo)

2

3

1

4

5

6

7

1

2

3

4

5

6

7

1   Kiki disappointed.
    (concept sketch by Katsuya Kondo)
2   Kiki delivers the pacifier for Osono.
    (concept sketch by Katsuya Kondo)
3-4 Kiki delivers the pacifier.
    (concept sketch by Shinji Otsuka)
5   Kiki timidly enters the bakery.
    (concept sketch by Yoshifumi Kondo)
6-7 Osono offers Kiki a cup of coffee.
    (concept sketch by Yoshifumi Kondo)

1

2

3

1   Osono. (character design)
2-3   Osono. (concept sketches)

"I didn't want her to be fat the way she was in
the original so she looks slimmer. She seems
strong-willed, sort of like actress Mayumi
Ogawa in her youth." (Katsuya Kondo)

4

4   Osono and her husband. (concept sketch)
5-6   Osono's husband. (concept sketch)
7   Osono's husband. (character design)

"There's no need for Osono's husband to speak in this story. Kiki probably wouldn't pay any attention to him if he spoke anyway. The husband is in fact concerned about her, but he's just not the gregarious type. Kiki also isn't comfortable speaking with a full-grown man. So we ended up with a film that's almost entirely feminine. Of course, there's Tombo who's not really a man yet, behaving like a fool instead." (Hayao Miyazaki)

6

5

7

85

1

2

3

4

5

6

7

8

1   Bakery's main street. (concept art)
2   Bakery at night. (concept art)
3   Back of the bakery.
    (concept art/rough draft)
4   Bakery backyard. (concept art)
5   Backyard seen from Kiki's room.
    (background)
6   Back view of bakery. (background)
7   Bakery seen from slope.
    (background)
8   Bakery seen from slope.
    (concept sketch by Katsuya Kondo)

"The bakery was based on the
setting, but we didn't really
encounter any wooden structures
during our research trip. I was
impressed by the chimneys that
turn with the wind direction so I
used that for the bakery chimney."
(Hiroshi Ono)

1

1 Attic room. (background)
2-3 Attic room. (concept art)
4 Kiki shown to the attic room.
   (concept sketch by Yoshifumi Kondo)

"My drawings of Kiki's room were based on
Yoshifumi Kondo's pencil sketches. At first we
went with a wooden bed, but it looked too
shabby so we gave up that idea." (Hiroshi Ono)

4

2

3

1

2

3

4

5

6

1   Kiki in her pajamas. (character design)
2   Kiki in a camisole. (concept sketch)
3   Kiki in her pajamas. (concept sketch)
4-6 Kiki's day. (concept sketch by Yoshifumi Kondo)

"Depicting everyday life in animation can be
difficult or easy depending on how much you
like that kind of work. Because I began as an
animator I find it grueling. It's endless too."
(Hayao Miyazaki)

1

2

1-2   Kiki's day. (concept sketch)
3   Kiki in a swimsuit. (concept sketch)
4   Kiki in her attic. (concept sketch)

The swimsuit was drawn for the
scene from the original story where
she meets Tombo at the beach.

3

4

1

3

2

4

5

6

7

1   Kiki observing the bakery kitchen.
     (concept sketch by Katsuya Kondo)
2   Kiki helping out at the bakery.
     (concept sketch by Yoshifumi Kondo)
3   Original Guchoki Bakery bread.
     (concept sketch by Shinji Otsuka)
4   Osono and her husband, busy at work. (cel art)
5   Kiki walks by the girls. (cel art)
6   Fashionable girls. (character design)
7   Kiki taken by the latest fashions.
     (concept art by Yoshifumi Kondo)

"I got all the gestures for the girls and Kiki
by observing the new female animators I was
training. Once women have the numbers on
their side, even going to the bathroom can
turn into a spectacle." (Hayao Miyazaki)

1

2

3

1-2   Maki, the customer. (cel art)
3   Maki. (concept sketch/rough)
4   Maki wearing a mini-skirt. (character design)
5   Maki. (character design/rough)
6   Maki seeks Kiki's help. (cel art)

"I wanted her to look like one of those slim actresses
from old European films." (Katsuya Kondo)

4

6

5

1

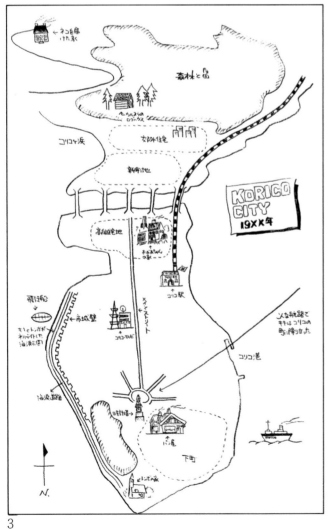

2

3

4

5

P. 100-101 Kiki flying above the city. (cel art)

1   Kiki examines a map of Corico. (cel art)
2, 4 Corico. (background art)
3   Corico. (rough sketch of map by Takesato Oaza/Hayao Miyazaki)
5   Kiki flying. (concept sketch by Yoshifumi Kondo)

1

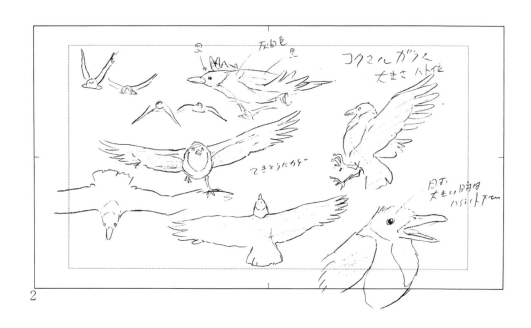

2

1   Kicking her feet up, Kiki freefalls. (cel art)
2   Jackdaw/crow. (character design)
3-4 As she chases after the falling birdcage, Kiki crashes
    into the trees. (cel art)

"She may be free when she's flying around, but she
has to learn how to be comfortable in the city without
relying on her broom and cat." (Hayao Miyazaki)

3

4

1

2

3

4

5

6

7

1   Kiki has Jiji make a delivery. (cel art)
2   Ket. (concept sketch by Yoshifumi Kondo)
3   Ket's mother. (character design)
4   Kiki gets Ket's mother's signature. (cel art)
5-6 The old dog Jefferson and Jiji. (cel art)
7   Jiji explains, "My friend, Jeff, helped me escape." (cel art)

"In the original script, the old dog was only supposed
to chase Jiji around, but it didn't work, so I altered
this scene at the storyboarding stage. A 12-year-old
dog would hardly be interested in chasing a cat."
(Hayao Miyazaki)

1

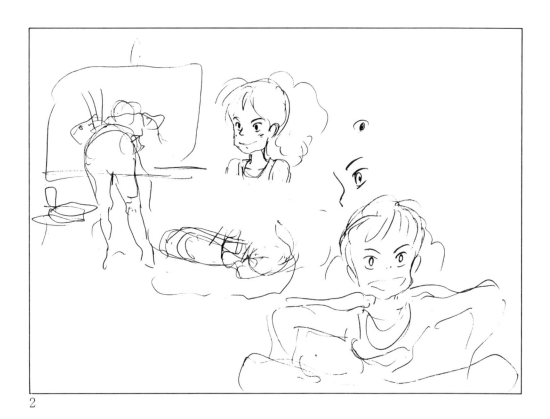

2

3

4

5

6

7

8

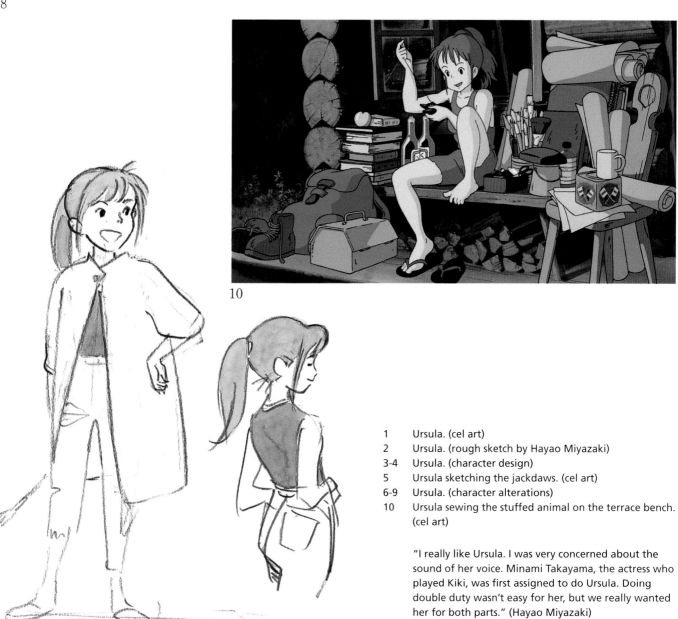

10

9

1   Ursula. (cel art)
2   Ursula. (rough sketch by Hayao Miyazaki)
3-4 Ursula. (character design)
5   Ursula sketching the jackdaws. (cel art)
6-9 Ursula. (character alterations)
10   Ursula sewing the stuffed animal on the terrace bench. (cel art)

"I really like Ursula. I was very concerned about the sound of her voice. Minami Takayama, the actress who played Kiki, was first assigned to do Ursula. Doing double duty wasn't easy for her, but we really wanted her for both parts." (Hayao Miyazaki)

1

2

3

4

1   Kiki tends shop. (cel art)
2   "Boring." Kiki is bored. (cel art)
3-8   Kiki apathetically addresses Jiji. (cel art)
9   Tombo chats with Kiki. (concept sketch)

9

5

7

6

8

1

2

3

4

1   The potpie lady's mansion. (background art)
2-4   Vicinity of mansion.

1

2

3

4

5

6

1   Kiki and the lady with the potpie. (cel art)
2   The old maid Barsa. (cel art)
3   The lady with the potpie. (character design)
4-5   The lady with the potpie. (concept sketch)
6   Kiki and Jiji help the lady. (cel art)

"She was a widow in the script, but Kiki really isn't mature enough to offer solace for a lonely woman. The 'odd couple' setup with another elderly woman solved this problem. I thought the sequence would work better to illustrate how Kiki makes friends." (Hayao Miyazaki)

1   The potpie girl. (cel art)
2-3 The potpie girl. (concept sketch)
4   The potpie girl. (character design)
5   Kiki delivers the pie in the rain. (cel art)
6   Kiki catches a cold from the rain. (cel art)

"In her line of work, Kiki's experience is hardly unusual.
Kiki learns the hard way how naïve she's been. She
thought she'd be appreciated. But that's not how the
real world works. She has to deliver the goods because
she's getting paid. You're lucky if you have a nice client.
Of course, she doesn't say this in the movie [laughs].
I like the way the potpie girl talks. It's very honest.
(Continued on page 119)

5

2

3   4

6

"She keeps insisting that she doesn't want a herring and pumpkin potpie. She really doesn't want it. Misunderstandings like this are very common, but they're hard on a girl like Kiki." (Hayao Miyazaki)

1   Kiki returning home in the rain. (film)
2-4 The bakery in the rain. (background art)

1

2

3

4

1

3

1   Inclined alley. (concept art)
2   Kiki descending the stairs of the shaded brick wall. (cel art)
3   Jiji and the white cat Lily. (cel art)
4   Kiki and Tombo meet again. (cel art)
5   Kiki impressed by the terrace view. (cel art)

"I don't really think Tombo and Kiki have become romantically involved at all. I do think, however, that they will become good friends." (Hayao Miyazaki)

2

5

1

2

4

3

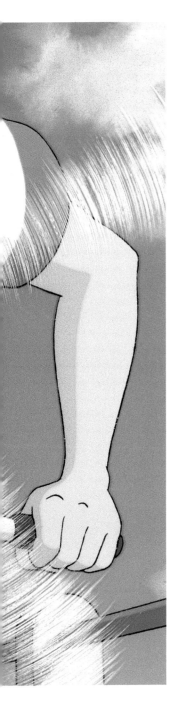

5

1-4 Tombo and his propeller bike. (cel art)
5 Tombo and Kiki riding the bike. (concept sketch by Katsuya Kondo)

"In this world flying isn't so bizarre, so flying bikes don't seem farfetched at all. I overlooked that original premise when I came up with this scene. Because the bike scene was all brushwork, it was very time-consuming. I thought we did a lot of shots, but the scene turned out so short. In any case, we needed a scene where Kiki really breaks out laughing." (Hayao Miyazaki)

1   Kiki chuckles with Tombo.
      (concept sketch by Katsuya Kondo)
2-3   Kiki and Tombo. Kiki bursts out laughing for the first
      time. (cel art)
4   Tombo and his friends/The potpie girl is sitting in the
      front passenger's seat. (cel art)
5   Kiki turns down Tombo's invitation. (concept sketch)

"Kiki knows she's too proud, but she doesn't know
what to do about it. That's part of adolescence. Even
if you know your opponent is right, you stubbornly
resist, resorting to some foolish act. Adolescence is
a crucial period. It's hard to overcome sometimes."
(Hayao Miyazaki)

1

2

3

4

5

1. Jiji approaching Kiki keeled over on her bed. (cel art)
2. Kiki notices how Jiji's changed. (cel art)
3. Kiki carves the yew stick as she weeps. (cel art)
4. Kiki tries to fly on her broom. (cel art)

"My concept of 'magic' in this film departed from the traditional approach to magic stories. I only wanted it to be a limited talent. So at times she won't be able to fly. It would've been pointless to explain, for example, how she couldn't fly because of her fight with Tombo. I thought that girls watching this would understand the film on its own terms. We sometimes aren't able to draw something that once came so easily. We might even forget how we learned to draw it in the first place. I really don't know how this happens." (Hayao Miyazaki)

1

2

3

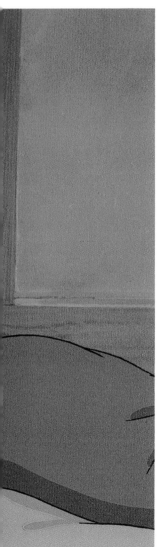

4

1

2

3

1   Ursula pays Kiki a visit. (cel art)
2   Ursula talks to Jiji. (cel art)
3   Ursula. (character design)
4   Ursula offers bubble gum to Kiki. (cel art)
5   Ursula on a shopping expedition. (character design)
6   Kiki hitchhiking with Ursula. (cel art)

"What Kiki really needs right now is a supportive
friend who'll visit her and understand her dilemmas.
Meeting someone like that is more important than
her vocation's status." (Hayao Miyazaki)

4

5

6

1

1   Ursula's painting. (photo drawing)
Background artist Kazuo Oga touched up and added Kiki's face to this print photo.

2   "Ship Flying Over the Rainbow," print. (illustration Xerox)

"It doesn't matter what Ursula paints as long as it's spirited. Given how her painting is thematically related to the film, the actual paintings had to be powerful. The paintings convey the life of a secluded female artist more than they do some message. I was looking forward to drawing them myself once I was done with the storyboards [*laughs*]. When I couldn't afford to do so, I recalled the print, "Ship Flying Over the Rainbow." The print was made by a teacher at a school for the disabled (Hachinohe City Minato Special Junior High School). We obtained permission from the instructor and added a face to the original illustration. Replacing the horse's face with Kiki's would have been inconceivable." (Hayao Miyazaki)

2

1

2

3

4

1 Kiki models for Ursula. (cel art)
2 Ursula sketches Kiki. (cel art)
3-5 Kiki and Ursula talk before bedtime. (cel art)

"She looks best when she's going through difficult times. Of course her happy face is appealing too, but it's important to emphasize her depth of character for both sides. Ursula wants to be Kiki's role model when she sees how dispirited Kiki is." (Hayao Miyazaki)

5

1

2

3

1   Kiki runs out of the tram. (cel art)
2-3 Kiki cries when she sees the cake inscribed with
     her name. (cel art)

"I was first looking forward to the scene where
she rides the tram, but we had to abbreviate it
with her only running out toward the mansion.
Of course, I have no idea why a tram would be
running through such a quiet area [*laughs*]."
(Hayao Miyazaki)

4

5

4-5 Kiki and the women riveted to the TV broadcast of the dirigible's accident. (cel art)

6 Worried about Tombo, Kiki dashes out. (cel art)

"Even a large scale accident looks more real on television. For the TV screen we applied transmitted light to our recently developed gray carbon to give it a washy look. The gray carbon created this effect." (Hayao Miyazaki)

1-2 Kiki frantically searches the city. (cel art)
3 Kiki borrows the deck mop from the janitor. (cel art)
4 Kiki concentrates while straddling the deck mop. (cel art)
5 Kiki flies as she guides the deck mop. (cel art)

"Given how her flying fails when she first arrives here, it was crucial to redeem her at the end. Otherwise, the film wouldn't resolve no matter how well she got along with the city's inhabitants. It's a rite of passage for her to fly over the city with her underwear exposed." (Hayao Miyazaki)

5

1

2

3

4

1

2

3

1   The Spirit of Freedom digs into the clock tower. (cel art)
2   The collapsed dirigible. (cel art)
3   Dirigible makes an emergency landing. (cel art)

"If this incident occurred in the first half of the story the film could have easily revolved around it. Given how it occurs at the end, the dirigible had to be peripheral throughout the story so that the final scene wouldn't be completely out of the blue. We also had to come up with various approaches like the television broadcast to make it seem more real." (Hayao Miyazaki)

1

2

3

1   Kiki rescues Tombo as she flies erratically. (cel art)
2   The crowd below cheers on Kiki and Tombo. (cel art)
3   Kiki surrounded by reporters as Jiji leaps onto her shoulder.
       (cel art)

"I wanted the film to leave the viewer with the impression
that no matter how dispirited she gets, in the future she'll
always rise above it. I didn't want to have a 'happily ever
after' ending where she achieves success in her vocation or
turns into a celebrity. I really didn't want to make it into a
job-success story." (Hayao Miyazaki)

1

2

144

3

4

5

6

7

8

9

10

1-9   Ending shots.
10   Her parents and Dora reading Kiki's letter. (cel art)

"I wanted the ending shots to be heartwarming.
I also wanted to include Osono's baby—It was
really crucial to show how Kiki has friends her
age and how she gets over her grudges. After all,
there isn't anyone particularly mean in this story."
(Hayao Miyazaki)

1

1   Panorama of Corico. (background art)
2   Closing shot/Kiki descends to the city on her deck brush. (cel art)

The panorama illustrations of Corico were drawn by Miyazaki.

2

Theatrical release poster. (Illustrated by Hayao Miyazaki.)

PART THREE
ANIMATION
TECHNIQUE

Animation processing for *Kiki's Delivery Service*

Written by Sunao Katabuchi

Sunao Katabuchi was born in Osaka on August 10, 1960. The assistant director of *Kiki's Delivery Service* was script supervisor for *Meitantei Holmes*.

1 Camera Movements (Camera Work)

What I mean by "camera" here isn't so much the actual camera shooting the cels and backgrounds but the process involved in shooting an imaginary world with live action cameras to create animation images.

Animation images are flat, but we need them to convey three-dimensional depth. It is very crucial then to have a good grasp of the camera's perspective.

◆FIX

The mounted camera remains fixed. This is self-explanatory.

◆PAN

Photo 1

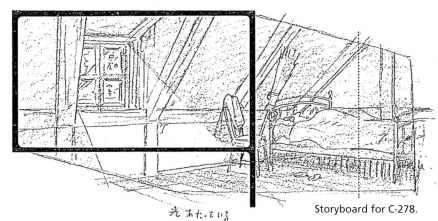

光あたっている

Storyboard for C-278.

Photo 2

The camera can be rotated if the image doesn't fit within the frame.

The technique is also applied to provide a sweeping view for wide images (the term "pan" came from panorama photography).

Because panning only involves rotational movement, the distant and close-up perspectives aren't mismatched the way they can be in a follow shot (which I'll address later). Every part of the perspective moves at the same speed in a pan shot. There is vertical panning as well. Photo 2 is Pan Up (P.U.) and the opposite is called Pan Down (P.D.).

◆Track Pan

Photo 3

This type of pan where we follow the moving subject is called Track Pan or Follow Pan.

The constant shift between the distance and the angles between the camera and the subject, combined with the fast angle shift (faster than the shift in a tracking shot) in the background art, animates the overall image.

Track Pan shots can also involve zooming. With this effect, the subject's size and angle remains unaltered, but the background moves very fast. Photo 4 is an example of this effect.

Photo 4

◆Follow Shot

Photo 5

Here the camera erratically follows Kiki's flight (photo 5). Follow movement involves following the subject. The shot angle on Kiki remains constant. As a result, the distant view doesn't fly by as it does with track panning.

From a train passenger's perspective, distant objects move slowly while closer objects move rapidly. In order to convey this relationship between speed and distance, we have to emulate the same effect. Photo 6 is an example of this effect (this example illustrates how P.O.V. shots are included in track shots).

The backgrounds were divided into several layers (with BOOK). The speeds for these portions were altered. We call this close multi-planing. ✱Note 1

Photo 6

Photo 7

The land and water are supposed to be receding at the same speed, but given how water reflects the sky above, we can make the movement look more real by making the water move slower than the land.

Photo 9

Photo 8

A follow shot of the dirigible. Everything besides the sky, including the TV and walls, was done with BOOK. The sky is the only background in this slide sequence. This is not called close multi-planing.

Sometimes a background cannot be divided into planes. As in the street in photo 9, when the image is continuous from front to back, we can only draw it as cel animation. This is called background cel animation.

Another example of indivisible backgrounds involves follow shots right in front or behind the movement. I'll address this later.

Note 1   Slide refers to the process whereby the cel, BOOK, or background is repositioned on the shooting table with each shot. For a straight slide, different speeds can be overlapped, but the number of overlaps is limited to the number of shooting tables available. If there are no overlapping speeds, then curve shots can be achieved as well.

At one third of 1/20 inch for each frame, the slide scale was extremely detailed for *Kiki's Delivery Service*.

◆T.I., T.B. (Track In, Track Back)

The term for tracking or "truck" comes from the use of camera trucks in live-action films.

For animation, it provides a simple technique to expand or shrink part of the image (photo 10).

In this shot, Ursula's painting gradually fills the screen. This is Kiki's point of view and we want her to be enveloped by the image. The camera merely closing in on the painting isn't enough. We're looking for an effect similar to a live-action film zoom shot.

Then how do we achieve this approach effect?

Let's consider the train example. The analogy we might draw is the driver's P.O.V. at the front of a train. As the camera moves forward, the perspective widens as if approaching the viewer. The distant objects move slowly while the immediate ones move fast. For Kiki's Delivery Service, given how we express the young girl's feelings by depicting her perspective, this type of camera work is absolutely essential. Let's look at some examples.

Photo 10

We did Track In or Track Back, with close multi-plane processing for the background (photo 11).

Photo 12 provides an example of a complete tracking shot applied in order to preserve the size of a character in the foreground. Only the background is multi-planed with a T.B. shot while the characters are inserted with optical montage. ✳ Note 2

Note 2   Optical montage is a process whereby separate film negatives are combined in the film lab to form a single image.

Photo 11

Photo 12

Photo 13

Photo 14

We can also turn the entire image, including the background, into an animation cel (photos 13 and 14). However, the drawing process would be labor-intensive and—due to the cel painting involved—the colors might not match with the previous and subsequent shots. Given these factors, the sea, which didn't require movement, remained a background image.

Distant objects don't change much even when the camera moves. So for long shots, only the nearer objects require background animation. Of course, we need to add T.I. (or T.B.). Otherwise the long view would look completely static (photo 15). In addition, photo 16 incorporates close multi-planing.

Photo 15

Photo 16

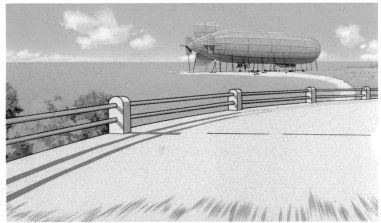

Photo 17

Panning is applied for curving shots, so the background quickly drifts to the left (photo 17). Because there isn't anything approaching the camera directly, the effect can be achieved without any T.I.

This method was utilized in the bus departure shot in photo 18. The view outside is supposed to expand, but we omitted this aspect because it would require optical montage. It turned out surprisingly well though.

Photo 18

Camera work often involves combined techniques. An extreme case would be this shot in photo 19. Side-tracking from the top of the train, the camera then pans and captures the forward movement.

It first begins with close multi-planing. As the camera pans, the shot turns into background animation. Finally, the background's horizontal movement is achieved by BOOK slides.

Photo 19

Photo 20

◆Multi-Plane

Animation images are mostly in panoramic focus; in other words, they're almost entirely in focus. But when there's an extreme close-up, it's best to blur the subject or the background. We only used multi-planing for this approach in *Kiki's Delivery Service*. The shot in photo 20 conveys the constricted feel of the place.

Photo 21

2 Transparency, Expressing Light and Shadow (Multi-Exposure)

Animation images are more than drawings. They have to be filmed. By utilizing film techniques we can expand our expressive possibilities.

Photo 22

◆Double Exposure

What would happen if you rewound what you filmed and shot something over this footage? You might expect some kind of doubling effect, but due to the over exposure the entire image would be erased. So instead we reduce the exposure by half, rewind the film, and then shoot again at the same reduced exposure.

We produced the shot in photo 22 by applying this multiple-exposure. At first we only shot the sky and the chimney without smoke, then we shot them again with cel images of smoke. This smoke consisted of opaque cels, but because it was double exposed with the sky it looks transparent. In fact the entire image is doubled, but you can't tell because everything besides the smoke was perfectly overlapped.

That's double exposure in a nutshell.

You can make half-transparent images like the shot in photo 23. The spinning propeller in photo 24 and the lace curtains in photo 25 were also created using double exposure. Double exposure works well when we need to add transparency and presence to the image.

The first exposure and second exposure don't need to be identical. The ratios can be anything from 4:6 or 8:2, as long as the total exposure is a normal value. Depending on the ratio, the transparency can go from light to extreme.

Photo 23

Photo 24

Photo 25

◆Dissolve Within Shot

By altering the double exposure with each frame, we can radically alter the rate of the dissolve. By changing the ratio from 1:0 to 0:1, we can also highlight subtle elements or conversely subdue prominent aspects.

Photo Sequence 26

Photo Sequence 27

We filmed the light coming in through the door in photo sequence 26 using a dissolve within the shot.

For the shot in photo 27, we created images where five different rays were shifted throughout the overall image, either by repeatedly dissolving them within short shots, or replacing them.

When utilized effectively, we can convey light by using dissolves within a shot, even if the light source itself isn't visible. This kind of "reflection effect" can play a prominent role in expressing light.

◆Superimposition

Creating partial over-exposures is called superimposition. This process also involves double exposure photography, but we film the initial footage at full exposure. The second exposure involves painting cels for those parts that need to be overexposed. Everything else is masked because black doesn't register on film.

The sky reflected against the glass in photo 28 was overexposed.

Photo 29 illustrates a more complicated process. The buildings, people and cars reflected in the show window are all superimposed. The brighter spots within these objects are overexposed while the darker spots aren't visible. This is exactly how glass reflections work.

As long as the reflections are properly conveyed, there's no need to draw the glass itself.

Furthermore, we can apply superimposition for whitish, half-transparent objects. More specifically, we can use it to express various lighting effects and rays.

In photo 30, we applied superimposition for the rain, train light, and the projected ray of light.

We used a real light called transmitted light for the ray of light here. We cut out the luminous parts from black paper or the cel, and superimposed the area lit from behind like shadow puppets. It gives a distinct tinge to the lighting.

Transmitted light can blend into all kinds of colors (photo 31). We can apply cellophane-like filters like colored paraffin. The same concept is used in shadow puppet plays.

Photo 28

Photo 29

Photo 30

Photo 31

We also used transmitted light for the TV image in photo 32. Everything on television drawn in black and white was shot normally. Then a weak transmitted light emulating the screen was superimposed to give a pale blue glow to the screen. We created the scan lines by applying half transparent gray horizontal lines while shooting the transmitted light in order to reduce the lighting in these areas.

Photo 32

◆Half Exposure

As opposed to superimposition, half exposure involves the under exposure of certain areas. The process is identical to double exposure photography. The image is underexposed in the first shot. For the second exposure, the darker areas are masked with black cels. The masked areas aren't exposed so the underexposed image remains intact.

Photo 33

Photo 34

Photo 35

Photo 36

We can apply this process to make shadows move over the background as illustrated in photo 33 of the shadow on the pavement. It can also be applied to convey the oozing in the carpet in photo 34.

Finally, I'd like to point out some examples where we conveyed transparency, light and shadows without using the above photography techniques. The flask in photo 35, the transparency of the lamp shade in photo 36, the light on the cow in photo 37, the puddle in photo 38—these were all produced by color coded cel painting. Photo 36 included a little bit of airbrushing. We used transmitted light for the headlights in photo 39, but neither superimposition nor double exposure were used to produce the reflections off the other freight train and train tracks. We simply produced them through our close collaboration with the animators and color design staff.

Photo 37

Photo 38

Photo 39

Other Terminology:

Rolling

Miniscule, repetitious vertical movements of the character to convey floating, unstable action such as flying. When the background isn't tracked, additional rolling can be applied to the background in order to destabilize the static background.

Image Movement

Utilized to convey a blow or other collisions. A frame-by-frame vertical movement is applied to the entire image. Viewed on film, this effect shakes the entire image.

Coach Jostling

Precise rolling where the vertical movement occurs frame by frame. It was originally used to emulate the movement of horse coaches, but the term isn't widely used now.

F.I.F.O. (Fade In, Fade Out)

During a scene change sometimes the screen will turn dark and then light up (this tends to occur to signify a break in the story).

The darkening process refers to F.O. while lighting up refers to F.I. We can create a dissolve by rewinding the film after an F.O. and overlapping an F.I.

From top:
Rolling
Frame Movement
Coach Jostling

1   2   3

4   5

Strobe

Constant repetition of shot within shot dissolves.

Even if we'd resorted to hand drawing and paintings, it would have been difficult to convey the slow movement of the serene lake waves emerging and receding so we ended up applying strobe effects.

PART FOUR

THE COMPLETE SCRIPT OF THE FILM

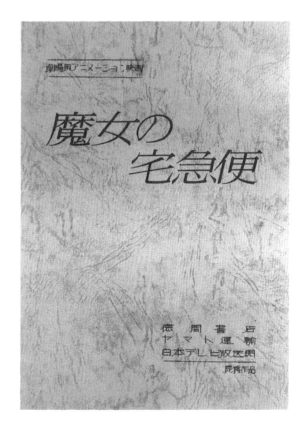

KIKI's DELIVERY SERVICE

Film Screenplay

This film transcript is based on the English subtitles translated from the Japanese dubbing script. All the dialogue is identical to the final version, including lines altered during the dubbing sessions. Furthermore, all personal names and stage directions have been unaltered.

Here is a brief glossary for film terms used throughout the screenplay:

Fade In	The frame lights up gradually.
Pan	Horizontal camera movement on an axis.
Pan Up	Upward camera movement on an axis.
Pan Down	Downward camera movement on an axis.
O.O.F.	Out of Frame. Indicates the subject moving outside the frame.
I.F.	Into Frame. Indicates the subject entering the frame.
S.E.	Sound Effect.
T.B.	Track Back. Camera moves back.

Previous page: Cover of voice-over script for the dialogue and characters' movements based on Miyazaki's storyboards.

Grassy Knoll

FADE IN
Clouds drift over the lake. The lake waves shimmer. Pan across the forest, houses, fields, and farms on the far shore to Kiki lying on the grassy knoll. The grass blows in the wind.

MAN ON THE RADIO: We've been receiving so many calls, asking about this marvelous airship, the *Spirit of Freedom*, which, uh, may or may not be passing over our area soon. I'll let you know as soon as we have more information available.

Kiki gazes at the drifting clouds. Her hair, ribbon, and skirt rustle in the wind.

MAN ON THE RADIO: But, first, here's the weather forecast. Skies are clearing up, thanks to a high-pressure front moving in from the mountains. Mild winds will be blowing in from the west...

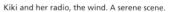

Kiki and her radio, the wind. A serene scene.

MAN ON THE RADIO: There'll be a beautiful full moon lighting up the skies...

Clouds rush by. White flowers rustle. Bees buzz by.

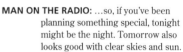

Kiki appears to be sleeping. A nice breeze. The weather forecast ends, followed by the business market update.

MAN ON THE RADIO: ...so, if you've been planning something special, tonight might be the night. Tomorrow also looks good with clear skies and sun.

Kiki gradually opens her eyes. She reaches for the radio and turns it off. She gets up with her hand on the radio. The wind blows by.

-pause-

She stands up and walks in the upper right direction. She walks O.O.F. into the distance. She doesn't have an urgent look, but she does seem preoccupied.

Fence

There's a fence between the farms. Water drips down. Mud with cow hoof prints. Kiki descends the far slope, skips over the water from the fence opening and makes a shortcut to the front right.

Road

The village road (downward slope). A man riding a bicycle. Kiki dashes out from the row of trees. They pass by each other, exchanging greetings. Kiki runs to the front left.

Top of the Hill

Center of the village. Kiki climbs up the hedge road to the top of the hill that looks down on the lake bridge. She ducks through the shortcut of the hedge and enters the flower garden.

Okino Residence/Garden

Flowers sprawled all over. An array of medicinal herbs and plants. Butterflies flutter by.

Okino Residence/Interior

Entrance covered with ivy. Jiji is taking a nap. Kiki runs in and exclaims.

KIKI: Jiji, wake up!

She slows down, but continues yelling as she goes O.O.F. toward the sunroom.

Jiji drowsily opens his eyes, and then stands up, bewildered.

JIJI: …?!

Okino Residence/Sunroom

Interior of sunroom. The array of plants reveals her mother's taste. Kiki leans in through the window and shouts.

KIKI: Hey, Mom!

She notices something on her right.

KIKI: Oh.

The room is filled with medicinal herbs and dried flowers. Kokiri is too preoccupied with her work to talk. The woman who turns around amongst these plants is an old woman. Kiki notices her.

KIKI: Hi, Miss Dora.

But then she immediately turns to Kokiri.

KIKI: Hey, Mom, it's gonna be clear tonight.

Kokiri carefully prepares her potion. Kiki leans in.

KIKI: And guess what. The radio says there'll be a full moon!
KOKIRI: Did you borrow your father's radio again without asking?

Kiki is nowhere in sight by the time Kokiri has finished mixing her potion.
She's rushing through the entrance hall and runs into a room full of herbs and bottles. The expression she's wearing now is in sharp contrast to the pensive look she wore on her way over here.

KIKI: Don't worry. He doesn't mind.

She runs up to Kokiri still at work and curtsies, tugging her skirt hem.

KIKI: Please excuse me, Miss Dora.

Like an only child, she immediately asserts her decision.

KIKI: Mom, it's a perfect midnight for me to leave home.

Kokiri turns to her.

KOKIRI: You mean tonight? Next month is what you told me.

Kiki, too impatient, cuts her off.

KIKI: Yeah, but the next full moon might be on a cloudy night. And I want to leave on the perfect midnight.

Like an infant, she rushes off O.O.F. once she's had her say. Slow to respond, Kokiri calls after her.

KOKIRI: Huh? But, Kiki! Wait!

Then the flask in her hand suddenly bursts.

(S.E.) BOOM

With a cloud of black smoke the flask is cracked.

KOKIRI: She takes a deep sigh.

KOKIRI: Uhh.

Dora continues smiling.

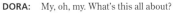

DORA: My, oh, my. What's this all about?

Kokiri glances over at Dora. She crouches, tosses the ruined flask into the bottle container and stands up.

KOKIRI: It's one of our oldest customs that when a witch turns 13…

She takes another flask and medicine bottle and prepares her potion again.

KOKIRI: …she has to leave home for a year to begin her training.

Kokiri mixes the potion. Dora remains cheerful.

DORA: Your little baby is 13? My goodness, but time flies so quickly.

KOKIRI: I know. She seems so young to be leaving home now.

Kokiri is worried about Kiki.
Dora rises with a kind smile.

DORA: I remember very well the exact day you arrived in this town.

Kokiri glances toward Dora.

DORA: (O.O.F.) A little girl flew down from the sky on her broomstick. And, I was certain she was much too young to hold such an important job as resident witch.

Kokiri almost chuckles, but performs her magic instead.

(S.E.) POOF!!

The potion sparks and erupts into a cloud of smoke. Dora seems to be recalling something funny, probably some absurd incident. Kokiri on the defensive. (O.O.F.) Bottle tapping.

KOKIRI: (O.O.F.) Yes, but I could fly. Kiki barely knows how to do that.

Kokiri pours the medicine into a bottle, and enters frame sitting beside Dora.

KOKIRI: And, I have had no time to teach her how to mix potions like me.

She slides the bottle of potion over to Dora.

DORA: Hmm. Young people are all the same. They all want to do something different.

She leans over and pats Kokiri's arm.

DORA: But, I hope, you at least get to teach her the potion that cures my rheumatism.

KOKIRI: Ha ha…

Kokiri offers a warm but bittersweet smile.

Kiki's Room

Sound of the radio. Kiki packing her bag on the floor.

KIKI: Hurry up! We always said we'd leave on the perfect night, didn't we?

She stands up, opens her drawers, and rummages through them.

Kiki's lower body takes up part of the frame. Jiji is on the floor. The radio is right next to him.

JIJI: Uh-uh. Our plan was that we would stick around for another month and play it safe.

Kiki won't even stop to listen to Jiji. She dashes past him O.O.F. to the left.

KIKI: I liked that plan. And, if we put it off for a month, and I find some wonderful boyfriend, then what'll we do?

She quickly rummages through her drawers, retrieving her clothes, nudging the drawers shut with her ankle.

She skips by Jiji and throws her towel, clothes, and pajamas on top of her bag. Jiji still insists.

JIJI: I'm gonna put my paws together and pray you're not serious.
KIKI: Of course I am.

Kiki pushes aside the books on the shelf to retrieve her piggy bank. She rattles it by her ear and runs O.O.F.

(S.E.) KLAKK KLAKK.

KIKI: You know ever since I turned 13, I've been excited about making this trip.

She skips over to her bag. She quickly kneels down and stuffs everything including her piggy bank into her bag. A car screeches to a halt. Kiki turns.

KIKI: There!!

She stops packing and rushes O.O.F. to the right. She's ecstatic.

Window Exterior

Kiki leans out of the window and shouts.

KIKI: Dad! Dad! Guess what! I've decided to leave tonight!

Okino is standing on the foothold as he struggles to untie the luggage from the car roof. He tugs the rope and turns.

OKINO: You're...You're going away?
KIKI: Yeah, there's a full moon!

The news takes him by surprise. He steps off the car and looks up.

OKINO: Well, yeah, but what happened to the camping trip we were supposed to take this weekend?
KIKI: Sorry, Dad!

Kiki offers a casual reply and goes O.O.F. Okino glances up, then panics.

OKINO: Aah, oh. Uh, Kiki, wait!

Okino trips on dangling rope. His luggage falls off the roof onto the ground. The camp equipment scatters.

(S.E.) KLANG KRRSH!

Okino recovers from his disheveled state. He turns around anxiously then runs O.O.F. toward the house.

First Floor

Inside house. Pan from the stairs.
Okino's voice. He's talking on the telephone.

OKINO: Ye-Yeah, I'll expect you then. Thanks.

Holding the receiver, he immediately dials another number. He speaks again. He seems to be contacting his relatives and close friends.

OKINO: Hi, Mom, it's me. I wanted to make sure you knew that Kiki is leaving tonight. Yes, midnight.

Kiki's Room

Kiki wearing a newly sewn dress. She tries on the dress and buttons up the back collar. Kokiri glances at the mirror.

KOKIRI: Very pretty.

Kokiri kneels down and finishes up the sleeves. Kiki stares at herself in the mirror.

KIKI: Lilac would look prettier on me. Or white.
KOKIRI: Witches have worn this color for a very long time, Kiki.

Kiki stares at the mirror, fidgets with her ribbon, poses and frowns. Jiji also looks at the mirror.

KIKI: Oh, Mom, I look really dumb.

KOKIRI: It's not really important what color your dress is. What matters is the heart inside.

Kiki gives her mother an exasperated look then she turns to the mirror and puts her hand on her chest.

KIKI: Well, I'm gonna be the very best witch that I can be, Mom. And, I know having a good heart is important.

Kokiri stands up next to Kiki and gazes at the mirror with her.

KOKIRI: Just follow your heart and keep smiling.
KIKI: Yeah.

Kokiri takes another dress from the chair. She picks up her sewing box.

KOKIRI: And, be sure to write home as soon as you're settled.

As she exits, Okino enters. Kiki sees him in the mirror, turns around, and takes him by the hand.

KIKI: Dad! Oh. Can I please take the radio?

She leans on him and addresses her mother outside the room.

KIKI: Mom, didn't you say I could have the radio?

Kokiri stops descending the stairs, turns and nods.

KOKIRI: Mm-hmm.
KIKI: (O.O.F.) Yea!

OKINO: (O.O.F.) All right. It's yours already.

Kokiri observes them talking, then descends the stairs.

Okino sits down on Kiki's bed. Jiji sits next to him.

OKINO: Well, now. You certainly look very grown up. My little princess.

Kiki prepares to make a pose. She's ecstatic.

KIKI: ♪Tada ♪♪

She spins around. The hem rises.

Okino smiles at his beloved daughter.

OKINO: You look just like your mother, when she was young.

Kiki blushes all of a sudden. She shakes her head, then suddenly reaches out.

KIKI: Dad, can you lift me up high, like when I was little?
OKINO: Well.

He immediately understands her gesture. He gets up enthusiastically and walks up to Kiki in the middle of the room. He puts his hands under her arms, but realizes she's too heavy to be lifted from this position so he crouches down. Kiki almost reaches the ceiling as she waves her arms. Her father spins her. She's not very light, but she mimics a plane.

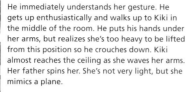

BOTH: Ha ha ha...

She's too heavy and lands on his chest.

OKINO: Oh...umph.

He holds her tightly. Kiki hugs her father by his neck.

OKINO: How come you never told me you were growin' up so fast?

Any parent can relate to this experience. He turns slightly then whispers gently.

OKINO: If things don't work out, you can always come home.

Kiki suddenly pulls back.

KIKI: And come back a failure? Oohaghh!

She makes a face.

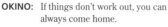

OKINO: Ha ha ha ha.

He stops laughing then looks at her kindly.

OKINO: Will you write us if you have the time?
KIKI: Mm-hmm. Oh, I love you, Dad.

Kiki smiles sweetly. Then she leans down. Father and daughter hug each other. Jiji watches them.

Moonlit Okino Residence

Pan over everyone seeing off Kiki by the entranceway. More people are showing up. Adults. The older guests are offered chairs.

MAN B: But aren't you worried about Kiki living in the big city all alone?

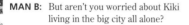

WOMAN B: Of course they are, but Kiki'll be just fine.

Kiki yakking away with her schoolmates. Kiki is all pumped up to go.

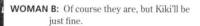

GIRL A: You're gonna find a city by the ocean?
GIRL D: Or maybe a town?
KIKI: Uh-huh. That's what I'm hoping, anyway.

GIRLS A, B, C: Wow. You're gonna have such a good time.
I'm so jealous.
You'll have so much fun!

Kiki sounds serious, as if offended.

KIKI: But I'm not going just for a good time. In order to be a good witch, I have to train a year away from home.

Girl A makes a wise crack.

GIRL A: Yeah. Be sure to tell that to the boys.

KIKI: TEE HEE...
OTHERS: Ha ha ha.

It's as if she's taking a school trip alone.
Everyone is watching Kiki.
Kokiri steps out with her broom.

KOKIRI: Kiki, it's time.

Everyone turns.
Kiki sprints over to the front right.

KIKI: 'Kay!

As her daughter approaches, Kokiri exclaims.

KOKIRI: That's the broom you're going to be leaving on?

Kiki shows her short broom to Kokiri.

KIKI: Yep! I just made it this morning all by myself.

Kokiri offers her big broom.

KOKIRI: Honey, it's too small to be really safe. I'd rather you took my broom. I know it better.

Kiki, disappointed.

KIKI: But, Mom, that one's so old!

Kokiri is unconvinced, but she's understanding.

KOKIRI: And, that's why it's good. You can rely on it time after time in any kind of weather.

Kokiri offers the broom to Kiki. Kiki is upset. She's too attached to her broom.

KOKIRI: (O.O.F.) Now, Kiki, do this for me, please.
KIKI: But I put so much work into this one. Right, Jiji?

She seeks Jiji's support.
Jiji glances up at her.

JIJI: Your broom is nice, but let's take your mother's.

Kiki is angry.

KIKI: You're no help!

Dora appeases her.

DORA: Now, Kiki, can't you make yourself another fine broom when you get settled down?

Kiki nods reluctantly.

KIKI: Mm-hmm.

Kiki turns to Kokiri who hands over her broom. The brooms are exchanged even though Kiki's still griping. Kokiri leans over and kisses her on the cheek.

KOKIRI: Be careful.

Okino's turn.

OKINO: You be strong, okay?
KIKI: I will!

She turns quickly and rushes to the left. She's not griping anymore as she moves O.O.F. Everyone sees her off.

Kiki runs up in front of the girls. She straddles the broom and prepares to launch amidst the girls' cheers.

GIRLS: Fly safely!
Girl! Go get 'em! Goodbye!

She winks at her friends and then looks ahead, building up her concentration. Her hair rises. Then her sleeves, skirt, hem all flap as she begins her ascent. The girls' cheering grows louder and louder.

GIRLS: Go, Kiki! Go, Kiki! Go, Kiki! Go, Kiki! Go, Kiki! Go!

She sways, then drops down. Kiki slaps the broom as if scolding it. (Tracking Pan) She zooms across the sky into the yard trees. The bells ring loudly.

(S.E.) KRRSH RRING RRING

She ricochets off into the night sky.
The bells on the tree ring.

(S.E.) RRING RRING

Kokiri and Okino gasp as they look after their daughter.

Kiki then flies toward the moonlit tree.
She crashes into it, making the bells ring again.

(S.E.) KRRSH RRING

She ricochets further back. She disappears behind the tree and then makes another crashing sound.

(S.E.) RRING

Everyone gasps at the sight. Kokiri is exasperated. Okino cups his ears.

KOKIRI: Aim your broomstick!

The bell ring recedes.

(S.E.) RRING RRING

Okino listens up.

OKINO: She'll be okay.
MAN B: I'm going to miss the wonderful sound of those bells.

The crowd turns silent. Okino puts his hand over Kokiri's shoulder. Man A nods. Kokiri gently wipes her moist eyes.

Village Sky

Kiki flies over the slope of village houses. She's accelerating. She still doesn't have total control. She's concentrating. Jiji shouts in the storm.

JIJI: Where are we going?

(PAN UP) They're both nervous and excited. Kiki shouts as if she's cruising on a motorcycle.

KIKI: I'm headed south to see the ocean!!

Kiki glides over the illuminated houses and heads toward the lake.
She sways in the air. Jiji screams.

KIKI: Jiji, climb up and turn on the radio. I don't think I can handle it. Can you do it?

Jiji reluctantly crawls under her arm and tiptoes over to the broom handle. The village recedes below, replaced by the lake. As the center of the village with the bridge passes under them, Jiji manages to turn on the radio. Music bursts out of it.

Kiki rocks abruptly, but then she floats up in response and moves O.O.F.

The starlit sky and full moon. Kiki comes in from the lower right and ascends to the upper right section.

The moon looks like a witch's symbol.
Main Title: Kiki's Delivery Service
(credits begin)

Sky Above the Lake

Kiki flies over the lake. She flies without her hands as if she's coasting. She rocks though and nervously grabs the broom, steadying it. She's happy and excited. The lights of the village across the lake sparkle.

The opposite shore slowly approaches. House lights below. The headlights of highway traffic are visible. Kiki flies by the church on the hill. The fields spread out below. The river zigzags. Glimmering house lights below.

Above the interstate at night. Kiki joyfully flies over the traffic of shining headlights and taillights. She is seeking "civilization."
A giant passenger plane covered with colored lights like a Christmas tree approaches. It flies right over Kiki. They're so close, it's as if she could almost hear what's going on inside the plane. She's impressed. She glances at Jiji for confirmation. Jiji is unimpressed.

The house lights glimmer below.
Under the starlit sky, villages and towns are scattered all over the earth like a nebula. The car lights flow down the interstate. The plane lights recede. Kiki flies in from the front right.

She flies over an industrial area. Factories operating at night. Part of the area glows from what appears to be a blast furnace opening up. Jiji curled up on Kiki's bag. He finds something and nudges Kiki. Kiki turns around. Jiji points out something. Kiki looks over and understands.

A fellow flying witch, Kiki's senior. She has a lamp on her broom.
Kiki descends toward her.

She flies down next to the unresponsive senior witch. Kiki talks to her enthusiastically.

KIKI: Hey. Good evening!

The senior witch calmly turns around as if she hadn't noticed Kiki until now.

SENIOR WITCH: It was!

She sizes up Kiki. The black cat also examines them.

SENIOR WITCH: You're new, aren't you?

Kiki rolls and replies as if to a varsity senior teammate.

KIKI: Yep! How'd ya guess? I just left home tonight.

The senior witch turns away, annoyed.

SENIOR WITCH: Uh-huh. Would you mind turning off that radio? I prefer to fly without being distracted.

Kiki rushes to turn off the radio. She ends up rocking and loses her balance, but then steadies her broom and continues flying with the senior witch. She tries to stay calm.

KIKI: Could you tell me? Is it really hard to get settled into a brand new city?
SENIOR WITCH: Oh, yes. A lot can go wrong.

The senior witch replies confidently as she calmly turns to Kiki.

SENIOR WITCH: But since my skill is fortune-telling, I can handle anything.

She feels so superior!!

Wow!! Kiki is impressed.

KIKI: fortune-telling?
SENIOR WITCH: Yes. I tell fortunes about love.
KIKI: Wow!

The senior witch smiles as she needles Kiki.

SENIOR WITCH: And what exactly is your skill?

The two continue talking as they roll.

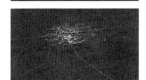

KIKI: Um, well, I haven't really decided that yet.
SENIOR WITCH: Ah. Well, I'm nearly finished with my training period. I'm going home soon to show off my new skills.

The illuminated flow of car traffic. They approach a small city on the interstate. It has motel-restaurants on both sides, pink, green, yellow neon flashing.

SENIOR WITCH: (O.O.F.) That's my town down there.

Kiki leans over to look.

KIKI: It's so big!
SENIOR WITCH: Yes. To you, I'm sure it looks big.

The senior witch turns to Kiki.

SENIOR WITCH: I hope you don't have too tough a time.
KIKI: Thanks!

Kiki turns to respond but the senior witch rapidly descends.

SENIOR WITCH: Ciao!

Kiki watches her continuing her descent.
The city resembles a large mall more than it does a motel-restaurant area. The senior witch rapidly descends from the upper left.

Kiki watches her. Jiji voices his resentment.

JIJI: Jeez, what a snob! And did you see that cat?

Kiki looks at him.

KIKI: What's my skill?

Thunder in the dark.

(S.E.) KRAKKL BOOM

It begins to pour.

KIKI: AIEEE.

Kiki screams and hurries down toward land.
Clouds and shadows flash with the lightning.

KIKI: What are we gonna do? We can't stay up!

Kiki flies down through the rainstorm. The thunder spark illuminates them, bleaches the sky, and deforms Kiki's shadow. Thunder strikes. Kiki finds something below.

KIKI: Hold on tight!

Red lamp blinking on the side rail in the woods.
The outline of a freight train. Lightning flashes and lights up the train.
Kiki winds down from the front right.
Lightning strikes again as Kiki approaches the train in the dark.

Back of the freight train in the rain. The red light is blurry in the rain.
Kiki enters from the sky. She skims above the train, realizing it's a freight train.
The sky lights up again.
Kiki barely skims over the train roof.

JIJI: Kiki, that opening is extremely small!

The sky lights up.
Kiki sees something ahead.

KIKI: 'Kay! Nice landing.

The train's half open lid glows in the dark with a weak thunder spark. Kiki enters from the front right. She halts above the opening and dives in (O.O.F.).

(S.E.) WHUD

Inside the Freight Train

The train is filled with hay. Kiki looks around and gets up. She grabs the roof lid and forces it shut.

(S.E.) KLAAK

She fluffs up the grass around her.
She shuts the lid. She wipes her brow and exhales.

KIKI: We better rest here until it's dry.

She swings her bag behind, picks up her broom and crawls to the left.

JIJI: Won't we get in trouble?
KIKI: Not if nobody finds us.

Jiji walks cautiously over the hay as if it might swallow him up.

Kiki enters frame from the corner. The hay net shakes a little. She finds a good spot there and puts down her bag.

KIKI: Oh, I'm soaked through down to the bone.

She takes off her clothes and spreads them beside her.
Jiji is still nervous.

JIJI: Hello?

Kiki lifts an armful of hay.

KIKI: Ahh! Mmm! This smells great!

She snuggles under this mat of hay. She takes off her left shoe, turns over, and kicks off her right shoe. She's completely covered.
Jiji also joins her (O.O.F.).

Railway

The lightning stops, but it continues raining on the freight train.
The distant sound of the train approaches.

(S.E.) RRRRRR

From the far end, a diesel train with shining headlights approaches. The light is reflected off the rails.

(S.E.) RRRRRR

The night train roars by the freight car. It enters the frame with its lights.

A beam of light runs over the fright train.

(S.E.) KLAKETTA KLAKETTA

The engine train's headlights turn on.
Its warning horn blares as it begins to move forward.
It accelerates slowly.
The freight train moves through the rain.
Kiki and Jiji are sound asleep inside the train.

Moving Train/Next Morning

I.F. The freight cars bathed in the morning light.
PAN UP Through the freight car side paneling, glimpses of cattle silhouettes. It turns out to be a cattle car.

Inside the Freight Car

The calves feed on the hay, pulling it out of the ceiling net. Some are chewing the hay.

One of them takes a mouthful. Kiki's bare foot is exposed.

KIKI: Yeoww!!

Kiki wakes up all of a sudden. Jiji leaps up, startled.

Kiki tries lifting her foot.

KIKI: Ahh! Ah!

The calves lick her foot sticking out of the net. Kiki's leg seems stuck.

KIKI: Aha! Ahahaha.

It tickles. She bursts out laughing. She struggles, then finally manages to pull her leg up. She sighs, then digs through the hay, poking her head into the hole.

The net shakes and her face appears. She's surprised.

KIKI: Oops! Sorry. We didn't mean to fall asleep in your breakfast.

Moving Train

The train bathed in morning light. The roof lid opens and Kiki sticks her head into the wind, gazing toward the light. The morning sea spreads beyond the farms. The trees pass by.

Kiki steps out excited. Jiji also shows up.

KIKI: Wow! Jiji, you've gotta come see the ocean. It's beautiful!
JIJI: Big deal. It's just a big puddle of water.

Jiji comments sarcastically. Kiki's subsequent scream alarms Jiji.

KIKI: (O.O.F.) Look! Up ahead!

The trees pass by the frame. As they rush by a city appears beyond the sea. Pan shows this train heading toward the city.

KIKI: It's a city, floating on waves! How lovely! I wonder if they have a witch there.
JIJI: Oh, great.

Kiki is enthusiastic. Jiji remains skeptical. The city in the morning light is approaching. The freight train continues moving.

(S.E.) FWEEE RRRRR

The freight train crosses the steel bridge.

(S.E.) RRRRR RRRRR

As the train rattles through the steel arches, Kiki stands up on the roof. She straddles the broom in the wind. The steel bridge is cut off.

KIKI: Here we go.

Kiki quickly rises. She dances on the wind, floating like a leaf and then flying off to the upper left corner.

In the Air

Kiki ascends like a leaf in the wind. She steadies her balance and addresses Jiji.

KIKI: You okay back there?
JIJI: Fine.

Jiji finally says something. Kiki looks at the city.

She seems to be cruising, but she shakes the front end of the stick as if scolding it. She descends towards the ocean.

Sea

She descends towards the waves, entering the frame where a flock of seagulls fly over the sea. Kiki flies to the front left (O.O.F.). She glides over the surface. Seagulls flying around. The seagulls nearly graze her broom. Some flock together while others shoot off like arrows.
She approaches the city in the sun.

The seagulls take the lead. They approach the fishing boats coming out to sea.
Kiki waves at the fishing boats. The passing fishermen wave.
A bell tolls. Kiki looks ahead.

(S.E.) KLANG KLANG KLANG KLANG

PAN UP on the approaching harbor. A clock tower appears at the top of the city. It registers 8 o'clock. The rows of buildings tower over each other. The seagulls fly around.

The sight excites Kiki. She looks up at the clock tower.

KIKI: Wow! A clock tower. Look at this city! A place like this would be great to live in.
JIJI: But there may be some witches living here already.

KIKI: And, there may not be.

The harbor lighthouse recedes. Kiki is enthusiastic, but Jiji is skeptical.

Fishing Harbor

Bustling harbor. Hauling fish. Working men carrying the boxes of loaded fish. The cargo boat sets off slowly. Kiki flies over it. She rises above the fishing harbor. Small figures of workers and bicycles.

Kiki flies over the rooftops. She approaches the clock tower. With the sudden rush hour noise, she comes upon the central square traffic circle.

Central Square

(S.E.) RRRRRR

A flood of cars. People flowing in and out. Kiki stops.

She in midair, amazed at the sight.

(S.E.) VRRRRMMM

Rush hour in the city.
Crowds in the square, the market and bus stops. Buses moving up and down. Buses slowly departing. The flow of traffic.

The sea in the distance, fish shop, grocer, etc. Swarms of people.

Panorama of the square. Flow of traffic.
Kiki and Jiji floating in front of the clock tower.

KIKI: Look at how many people there are!
JIJI: Too many, if ya ask me!

(O.O.F.) The clock tower keeper.

KEEPER: Bless my hourglass. It's a real, live witch!

Kiki notices him. (TRACK PAN) The keeper is looking at her.
Kiki approaches the display. She's still looking to her side.

KIKI: Good morning! Do any witches live in this town?

The old man's reply is matter-of-fact.

KEEPER: Why, uh, nobody's seen one around here in a long time.

Kiki looks at Jiji.

KIKI: That's great! Our trip is over. We're staying right here.

Her heart's set.

KIKI: Thanks, mister! Bye!
KEEPER: Uh, no problem!

Kiki waves at him, turns and descends (O.O.F.).

Main street leading down from the center. Tram and cars. Kiki flies over the overhead wires.

She cruises by, ogling her surroundings. Jiji remains skeptical.

JIJI: Tell me we're not landing down there.
KIKI: Well, of course we are!

The intersection. Pedestrians waiting for the signal to change. Cars passing, cars idling, pedestrians walking, more cars. Kiki circles around to the shopping district.

Kiki drifts over the pedestrians. Some notice her and look up, while others don't. Kiki goes O.O.F. The pedestrians from Kiki's perspective. She relishes their attention.

Overly self-conscious Kiki. Jiji climbs up and panics.

JIJI: They're looking at us.
KIKI: I know. Smile, so we make a good impression.

A tourist couple gawks at her.
Tombo and his friends look up, too.
Kiki tries to glide along casually in the midst of this attention. She flies toward the overpass.

She turns from the sidewalk and enters the tunnel. Suddenly a double-decker bus enters.

KIKI: Uhh—Whoa!

She panics and stops. The bus rushes at her. Kiki dodges it, shakes like a leaf to the front left.

Kiki is blown to the opposite side of the tunnel. She's about to land, but a car screeches by and enters the frame.

(S.E.) KREECH

Kiki barely dodges it when a taxi comes screeching by and enters the frame.

(S.E.) KREECH

Kiki is blown away by the windblast.

Kiki escapes to the opposite side of the road. Then a chorus of cars screeches to a halt.

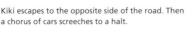

(S.E.) KREECH BEEP BEEP KREECH

CROWD: Whoaaaa!

Pedestrians dodging, freezing. Kiki goes O.O.F. into the ruckus. She winds through the crowd.

KIKI: Whoaaaa!
CROWD: Hey, watch out!

Long shot of the scene. Cars keep coming, screeching. People panicking.

(S.E.) BEEP BEEP KREECH
　　　　BEEP BEEP

Kiki emerges from the crushing wave of people. She frantically flies to the front. As she winds off the center of the frame she goes O.O.F. The crowd watches her.

Intersection

She turns the corner and escapes in a frenzy. She stops in the air, worried about the ruckus and descends on a corner. Pedestrians wait to cross the street. Kiki quickly gets off her broom. She's nervous, her eyes wide open.

People look exasperated. People walk off in the back and cars pass by.
Kiki is completely tense.

KIKI: …

She nervously shifts her broom and puts on her best smile.

KIKI: Um, hi! My name's Kiki, and I'm a witch. And this is Jiji. He's my black cat. And we'd be honored if we could live here.

She introduces Jiji and bows.

People gaze at her. There are also businessmen who simply pass by, and others waiting for the signal to change. Kiki stands upright and smiles. She enthusiastically announces her arrival.

KIKI: Your city is so amazing. And what a beautiful clock tower.

The signals change while she talks. Pedestrians cross the street. A kindly woman hesitates, then approaches Kiki.

WOMAN: Ohhh, really. That's very nice, dear. Bye.

In spite of her smile, she walks off, crossing the street. People come her way.
Kiki wants to stop everyone, but she's speechless. She finally understands how dismal the situation is. People pass by her. She's completely ignored.

A policeman strides in.

POLICEMAN: Hey, you kid!

The policeman stops. Kiki turns but then freezes. Jiji glances over.

POLICEMAN: Who do you think you are, jumping out into the street like that?

He looks intimidating. Others glance at him, then scurry off.

POLICEMAN: You were almost responsible for a big accident, zooming around on your broom back there.

Kiki desperately defends herself.

KIKI: But I'm a new witch, sir. We're supposed to fly around.

POLICEMAN: You're supposed to obey the law. I'm gonna write you up.

He pulls out his handbook from his pocket.

POLICEMAN: Now give me your name and address.
KIKI: Will you tell my parents?

Kiki in a tight spot.

POLICEMAN: Of course I'm going to tell your parents! I have to do that with every minor.

Someone shouts.

TOMBO: (O.O.F.) Thief! Thief!

The policeman stops and turns. The shouting continues.

TOMBO: (O.O.F.) Thief!

The policeman runs to the corner.

POLICEMAN: Hmm?

He stops and looks back at Kiki.

TOMBO: (O.O.F.) Somebody, call the cops! He's gettin' away!
POLICEMAN: Now you stay right there!

He mutters and runs off. Petrified, Kiki listens up. The policeman's footsteps recede. Kiki sneaks away O.O.F.

Tunnel

Kiki turns at the tunnel and walks away. Jiji leaps down.
Kiki appears calm, but she's trotting away O.O.F. They descend a slope leading to a back street. Unlike the main street it's empty. Kiki enters the frame as she walks on the right sidewalk. She goes out into the light.

Back Street

Kiki trots away. Jiji joins her. He's worried about walking off like this though and looks up at her.

Kiki from Jiji's perspective. She looks intense as she walks away. Jiji addresses her.

JIJI: Kiki, he said to stay here.

No reply.
Sirens.

(S.E.) EEYOO EEYOO

Jiji turns around.

(S.E.) EEYOO

Tombo fully enters the frame behind Kiki and Jiji walking away. Jiji hides behind Kiki's right side. Tombo addresses her as he comes up beside her. He's brazen like any city kid.

TOMBO: Hello?

Kiki glances over. She won't stop walking.

TOMBO: Miss! Wait up! I sure fooled that cop, huh?

Kiki marches forward. Tombo declares proudly.

TOMBO: Hey, that was me yellin' "thief."

Tombo remains oblivious to Kiki's aloofness.

TOMBO: You gotta be a real witch the way you can fly that broom.

The two approach.

TOMBO: Do you think, maybe, you can teach me how to fly it?

BOY A: (O.O.F.) Hey, Tombo! Maybe you can sweep her off her feet with that broom.

Boys jeer. (PAN) Tombo's perspective to the right. A group of brats.
Tombo winds around, then shouts back.

TOMBO: Hey, shut up, all right?

They're friends. He answers while dodging a garbage can.

TOMBO: Whooa!

He rides without his hands and follows Kiki walking away.
He passes her.

He enters from the left towards the iron lamp, grabbing it with his left hand and looking over at Kiki.
Kiki marches on.

TOMBO: You know, miss, I love flying too. Could I see your broom?

Kiki abruptly stops. She glares over at him and retorts quickly as if cutting loose.

KIKI: Thank you for getting me out of trouble.

KIKI: But I really shouldn't be talking to you, and you wanna know why? It's very rude to talk to a girl before you've been introduced and before you know her name.

She looks away in anger and stomps forward O.O.F.
Tombo is speechless and stares at her.
Kiki walks away, furious. Jiji checks on Tombo, but trails after Kiki.
Tombo grins.

He steps on his pedal and follows after her. He sweeps into frame, and follows Kiki as she walks away. As he rides up to her he continues chatting away.

TOMBO: You're kind of old-fashioned, aren't ya? You sound like my grandmother.

The comment only angers her. She turns away.

KIKI: Just go away and leave me alone!

She dashes forward and turns into the right alley. Tombo's left behind, but he's undeterred. He immediately follows her.

Alley

Tombo enters the alley. He stops and gapes at Kiki.

TOMBO: Ohh!

Kiki ascends into the blue sky above the narrow alley. She's in the light.
Tombo is gleeful.

TOMBO: Hmm. What a cool witch.

Hotel

City hotel. Flowers adorn the windows.
Lobby. Front desk clerk and Kiki face each other.

DESK CLERK: Stay here tonight? I'm afraid I don't understand. Your parents are here with you, aren't they?

Kiki explains desperately.

KIKI: No, sir, I'm alone. I've come to this town because I'm a new witch in training.

Clerk smiles.

DESK CLERK: Do you have some identification?

KIKI: Oh, never mind.

Park

Western sunlight on this part of town. PAN DOWN from statue.
People gathered at the fountain. Kiki and Jiji to the side. Her packed lunch on her knees. Kiki is pensive. Jiji is eating. Once he's done he speaks up.

JIJI: Kiki, aren't you going to eat that?
KIKI: No, you can have it, Jiji.

Jiji looks around.

JIJI: Where are we going to stay tonight?

Police car siren approaching.

(S.E.) EEYOO EEYOO

Kiki looks up.

Police car approaches the street beyond the trees in the park and parks. Its headlights are on. Kiki grabs her sandwich.

KIKI: Let's go.

She takes her broom, rises and walks O.O.F. Jiji scrambles after her.

Slope

Evening. The backlit clock tower chimes in at 6 o'clock. Serene setting.

Kiki ascends the deserted street.

(S.E.) BONG BONG

Top of the Hill/Bakery Storefront

A small bakery on a cliff looking over the sea. Kiki approaches.
Pedestrians hurrying home and passing cars. It's quiet. Kiki approaches the brick railing on the cliff. She looks at the ocean below. She's lonely. Jiji enters from below.

PAN across the downtown district and sea in the rightward western sunlight. Flock of seagulls. Kiki despondent. Cars descend the hill.

(S.E.) VRRRMM

Jiji timidly looks at Kiki.

JIJI: Why don't we go find another town?
KIKI: …

He tries to reassure her, but Kiki won't respond. He ends up staring at the sea.

The large bellied Osono enters from the front right with sound of footsteps. She rushes beyond Kiki. Kiki turns around.

Osono shouts. She has something in her right hand.

OSONO: Hey there! Your pacifier!

Kiki looks down, too.

OSONO: (O.O.F.) Ma'am, you forgot your baby's pacifier!

View of the old district. The carriage turns the corner. Baby carriage vanishes into the shade O.O.F.

OSONO: Oh! Poor baby.

Osono stands back. Kiki looks at her. Osono squeezes the pacifier.

CLOSE on pacifier.

OSONO: (O.O.F.) Without this, the baby'll wake up and cry all the way home.

Osono looks around, then rushes to the right (O.O.F.). Kiki watches her.

Osono rushes back to the store. She opens the door and addresses her customers.

OSONO: I'm sorry, folks. But could you wait just a minute? I'll be right back.

She walks toward the slope (toward Kiki). Osono passes Kiki. Kiki looks at her.

KIKI: Excuse me. But would you like me to deliver it for you?

Osono stops.

OSONO: What?

She looks over Kiki.

OSONO: But…

Kiki turns toward the old district and enthusiastically proposes her idea.

KIKI: The woman with the baby carriage who just went around the corner. I could reach her in no time.

Osono taken aback. She examines Kiki, then replies cheerfully.

OSONO: Really? You'd do that?

She approaches Kiki and gives her the pacifier.

OSONO: Thank you so much.
KIKI: My pleasure.

Kiki takes the pacifier with her right hand, shifts her broom, and turns around to the right.

KIKI: Let's go, Jiji!

She grabs the railing and jumps up. (PAN UP) Kiki quickly straddles her broom. Jiji leaps onto her. Osono astonished.

OSONO: Oh! Oh, my goodness!

From this peculiar position Kiki lifts up into the air and goes O.O.F. beyond the railing. Osono is shocked.

OSONO: (O.O.F.) Oh!!

She is amazed. She rushes to the front right and leans over the railing, staring down. Kiki flies upward. Osono gapes at her. She leans back and cheers.

OSONO: Wow!

Downtown Alley

Kiki flies over the district in pursuit of the baby carriage.
She passes the carriage, turns and then descends.

MOTHER: Wow!

She lands smoothly and dismounts her broom.

KIKI: Sorry to surprise you, but the lady in the bakery asked me to return this pacifier.

She steps forward and offers the pacifier. The mother is speechless.

BABY: WAHH!

The baby shrieks out all of a sudden. His hand appears. Kiki and his mother look down. Baby is sobbing.

BABY: WAHHH!

Kiki's hand offering the pacifier. Baby puts it in his mouth.

BABY: AH AHH…

Kiki and his mother look at him and then smile at each other.

Bakery Interior

Last customers during the peak hour before dinnertime. Osono takes out change from the register and offers it to her customer.
(S.E.) DING

OSONO: Here you go.

She says to the old man who's next.

OSONO: Here ya go.
OLD MAN: Eh, I'd like one of those.

He mumbles, pointing to the shelf. Osono cordially replies.

OSONO: Yes, sir.

She sees Kiki at the entrance.

OSONO: Oh, hi there. Come in and wait a minute, will you?

She turns to grab the bread from the shelf. Kiki at the entrance. She opens the door for the customer and dodges her while entering the store. Shot over Kiki's shoulder as she watches Osono busily at work. She takes the bread from the shelf and offers it to the old man.

OSONO: There you are.

Her husband brings out the last batch of bread.

OSONO: All right. Thank you very much.

The next woman in line pays her. The old man turns to exit. He puts his hand forward, opens the door, and exits slowly. Osono's husband replenishes the shelves.

OSONO: (O.O.F.) Here you go. See you tomorrow. Bye.

Kiki watches. Then she looks down at the note in her hand. She glances up as she notices Osono approaching.

KIKI: …?!

Osono enters frame in front of Kiki. She opens the door for the slow old man.

OSONO: Now come back again!

She also lets out the lemonade woman, closes the door, and then smiles at Kiki.

OSONO: When I saw you fly off, I thought for a second I was dreaming!

Kiki offers the note.

KIKI: The baby's mother told me to give you this message.
OSONO: Hmm?

Osono reaches out and takes the note. She opens it and reads it quickly.

OSONO: "Thanks for returning the pacifier. Your new delivery girl is really quite special."

Osono smiles and smiles at Kiki.

KIKI: Well, I'll be on my way.

She accomplished her job…she gets ready to go. Osono leans over.

OSONO: Wait!

She puts her hand on Kiki's shoulder and insists.

OSONO: Wait a minute. I really must do something to show you my thanks.

Her husband taking out the bread from the shelves. Osono enters and stomps by.

-pause-

The husband exclaims.

HUSBAND: Huh?

Kiki follows her. She rushes over O.O.F. to keep up with her.
Osono turns into the hallway next to the bakery and climbs up to the kitchen.

OSONO: Over here.

Kiki follows her. She glances over at her workspace.

Kitchen

Kitchen with low ceiling. Steam from kettle. Osono enters and lifts the kettle.

OSONO: Sit down and relax.

She addresses Kiki as she goes to the front right.

OSONO: Would you like some hot chocolate?
KIKI: Okay.

She shakes the cocoa into a cup, takes the kettle behind her, and pours the boiling water in. She fills up the other cup.

Kiki a little reserved.
Osono's hand holding the coffee cup.

KIKI: Thank you very much, ma'am.

She rotates the cup handle for Kiki and offers a small bowl of milk.

OSONO: (O.O.F.) And this is for you, little guy.

Jiji is interested, but he's too timid to get on the table. He looks at the milk and Osono. Osono's hands and the milk bowl appear.

OSONO: So, tell me if I'm right.

She sits while stirring her cup.

OSONO: I'm guessing you're a witch in training.

She continues then takes a sip.

Kiki reservedly puts a sugar cube into her cup. She puts on a smile, but feels dejected.

KIKI: You're right! And I really love it here, but people don't seem to like witches in this town.

Jiji finally steps down and looks at Osono.

OSONO: Depends on the people. Now, take me, for instance.

Jiji leans forward. Osono is cheerful. Jiji cautiously approaches and begins to lap at the milk.

OSONO: I just met you and I know I like you.

She blinks at Jiji.

JIJI: …!!!

Jiji is terrified, his hair standing on end. Osono gives Kiki an encouraging look.

OSONO: So, tell me, whereabouts are you two staying?

Kiki glances up from her cup suddenly. She blushes and looks down at her cup.

KIKI: Uhh…

Osono smiles and makes an offer.

OSONO: Why didn't you tell me you have no place to stay? We have a spare room in the attic. You can use that.

Kiki is amazed. She stands up.

KIKI: You'd really let me stay with you?

Osono bursts out laughing.

OSONO: Why, of course! But we haven't introduced ourselves. My name's Osono.

KIKI: And I'm Kiki, ma'am. And Jiji here is my very best friend.

Kiki is overjoyed. Jiji's stunned.

Yard

In the dimming twilight, Osono crosses the yard and ascends the external staircase. Kiki follows her.

Attic Room

A dark attic room with a single window.

(S.E.) KLIK

The lock clicks as the door opens. Osono enters with a bucket and mop. Kiki follows, carrying a blanket and sheets, and looks at the premises.

OSONO: It's right up here, Kiki. It may need a little dusting...but I think you'll like it.
KIKI: Yes, ma'am.

Osono stands up straight and starts walking out.

OSONO: All right, then. Water and bathroom are downstairs. Give a shout if you need anything.
KIKI: Thank you.

Osono exits. The door is left open. Kiki watches her leave. She examines the room again. A somewhat harsh setting. White powder everywhere.

JIJI: This is...quaint.
KIKI: Jiji!

She finds a bed in the corner, steps onto the raised floor, and walks up to the bed. The bed only has a mattress. She taps on the bed with her broom. A cloud of dust.
Jiji stops, examines the powder on his paws and looks around.

JIJI: If you wake up tomorrow and find a white cat, it's me.

Window Exterior

Attic Room Window. Filthy glass. A figure moving behind. It opens up, dust all over.
Kiki looks around. Then she notices something and dashes in.

KIKI: Ohhh, Jiji, we can see the ocean from here!

The view. Sea at sundown. The laundry in Osono's yard flutters.

KIKI: …

Kiki sighs at the sight of the sea horizon. She's feeling blue. Jiji addresses Kiki.

JIJI: Can we look for a new town?
KIKI: …

Kiki gives a half-hearted reply. Jiji looks ahead. Then he notices something.

A neighbor watering her flowers on the window. A cat on the windowsill.

MAN ON RADIO: I think the excitement is building for the moment when the big blimp appears in our skies. So, we're gonna go to Scott live as he reports in from Freedom Base One.

The woman returns inside after she's done watering her plants. A black and white television inside.
The female cat frowns.
Jiji is incensed.

JIJI: Huh! Pardon me, Miss Snooty Cat!

Central Square/Night

The clock tower lit up in the night sky.
A car passes by, its taillights illuminated.

Front of Bakery

Empty street. The street lamps are lit. Dim lights behind the windows. An ambulance siren.

(S.E.) EEYOO EEYOO EEYOO

Attic Room

PAN on dim moonlit window. Kiki is lying on her bed. The radio plays quietly. Her bag is her pillow. Jiji is curled up.

Kiki has her eyes closed, but she can't seem to sleep. She opens her eyes and talks to Jiji as if addressing herself.

KIKI: Jiji, I've decided not to leave this town. Maybe I can stay and find some other nice people like Osono…

There's no reply. She looks over at Jiji who's fast asleep. Kiki reaches for the radio switch and turns it off. She pulls up the blanket and closes her eyes. Her first day of training comes to an end.

Next Morning

Early morning. City still asleep in the morning fog. A fishing boat goes out to bay.

(S.E.) GLUG GLUG GLUG

The sluggish sea.

Attic Room

Dim room. Kiki curled up and asleep. She grimaces, turns over and uncovers Jiji. She buries her head under the blanket. Then she gets up suddenly.

KIKI: …!!

Kiki looks around as if she can't tell where she is. The flour storage attic. The dim morning light through the window.

Kiki realizes where she is. With a deep sigh, she pulls up the blanket to fall asleep again.

-pause-

Her eyes open. She tries closing them again, but it doesn't work.
She gets up reluctantly.

Yard

The second floor door. Its knob turns, the door opens and Kiki looks out. She opens the door slowly and looks out.

The bakery yard in the early morning. Birds chirp. She pauses, then gently shuts the door. She quickly descends the staircase, crosses the yard, and goes to the bathroom.
The bathroom door. Water flushing.

(S.E.) FSSSH

Knob rotates. Kiki retreats and closes the door. She opens the door and sees Osono's husband emerge. He's ascending the stone steps to the front right.

The husband heads for the center of the garden. He stops and begins to stretch. As he cracks his neck, he approaches the shed, opens it and enters. The bathroom door opens and Kiki checks the premises. She slips out, closes the doors and dashes off.

She rushes to the stairs in her pajamas. She scuttles up to her room.

Attic Room

The door opens. Kiki slides in. She quietly closes the door. She freezes for a moment. Then she sighs and relaxes. Preoccupied, she walks to the right O.O.F.

Kiki counting out her money on her bed. Jiji looks up drowsily. She puts down a bill and examines the rest. Jiji wakes up.

KIKI: How much do you think it would cost to get a phone here?
JIJI: A phone?

Kiki gathers her bills.

KIKI: Yep. We're gonna need a phone.

Jiji is bewildered.

Attic Window

Window. The window rattles open. Kiki brushes her hair with her right hand. She seems to have an idea and vigorously brushes her hair.

Kitchen

Bakery starts early. Morning light finally shines on the roof.
The oven burner. Flames. Husband's hand tossing in wood for the oven. He tosses in another log from under his left arm, and quickly closes the lid.

Osono enters. Her husband slides the sheet of croissants into the oven. Osono carries the freshly baked bread O.O.F. Her husband moves quickly, lifting the next sheet onto the bread peel and sliding it into the oven again.

Kiki is looking in through the window. She moves to the right O.O.F.
Osono returns. Kiki opens the door and enters.

KIKI: Morning, everyone!
OSONO: Well, look who's up! Did you sleep well?

Osono continues moving the bread to the shop. Kiki approaches the racks.

KIKI: Yes. Oh, that smells good! Can I help out?
OSONO: Sure can!

Kiki takes a pan, and the husband slides the bread in. Kiki walks toward the shop, passing the door. Jiji watches and looks ahead.

The husband finishes sliding in the bread, shuts the lid, and props the bread peel against the wall. He sees Jiji.

HUSBAND: …

Their eyes meet. Jiji is intimidated.

JIJI: …!!

Unperturbed, the husband goes O.O.F. to the right.
He stands at his worktable and takes some yeast off the shelf. From an awkward position he swiftly pulls out a pan, spinning it on his fingers. He's very conscious of Jiji. Jiji stares at him.

The Shop

Kiki sets the bread in rows. Osono gathers the trays. She stands up, impressed.

OSONO: Ooh, a delivery business, huh?

Kiki lifts another loaf.

KIKI: Well, I really only have one skill and that's flying. So I thought a delivery service wouldn't be a bad idea.

She moves the bread over to the shelves. There's a twinkle in Osono's eyes.

OSONO: It's a great idea—Kiki's Flying Delivery Service.

Hall

Hall to the kitchen. Osono enters, too.

OSONO: And, since you're staying right here, I can be your very first account.

Osono's offer makes Kiki turn around below.

KIKI: You mean it! Oh, that's great!

She turns around and steps down to the kitchen.

Kitchen

Husband brushing dough with egg yolk. Jiji watching. Kiki runs in. As she retrieves the bread from the shelves, Osono also enters. Kiki hands the bread to Osono.

KIKI: I was planning on putting a phone upstairs.

OSONO: But a phone is so expensive.

The husband continues working without a word. Kiki takes out more bread.

KIKI: I have a little saved up already.
OSONO: Don't waste your money!

She turns in front of the stairs.

OSONO: What I think you should do is use our phone. You know it will take some time to get regular customers.

Kiki doesn't know what to say. How fortunate though! She's starting to cheer up.

OSONO: I'll make you a deal. Since I'm expecting a baby, I could use help. If you mind the store once in a while, I'll let you have the room and the phone.

Osono stands up and winks as if making a nice offer.

OSONO: And, I'll throw in a free breakfast, okay?

Kiki is overjoyed.

KIKI: Yeah! We've got a deal! I'm gonna work very hard for you.

She bursts out, then walks on, leaning forward. She ducks Osono's tray. Osono dodges her.

OSONO: Aiee!!

Kiki climbs the stairs. She turns around in the hall.

KIKI: Osono, you're the greatest!

She dashes out to the shop.

OSONO: HA HA HA HA…

She's bewildered, but then bursts out laughing. She walks toward the shop O.O.F. Her husband looks on.

The boys watch, then look at each other.
They stare at each other for a moment.

HUSBAND: …

-pause-

Husband suddenly winks.

Jiji is startled.

JIJI: …!!

He hides his face.

Storefront

Bustling morning. Pedestrians, shoppers, etc.
Kiki working inside behind the shop window.
Blurry reflections of buildings across the street,
pedestrians, and cars.

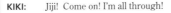

Attic Room

Kiki wiping the floor while listening to the radio.
Her skirt hem is soaked. She gets up and looks
around. She puts the mop into the bucket and
pulls down her hem. She looks out the window
and calls out.

KIKI: Jiji! Come on! I'm all through!

She runs O.O.F. She exits and addresses Jiji on the
rooftop.

KIKI: We're gonna go shopping. Come on!

She runs downstairs. Jiji leaps onto her shoulder
and they go O.O.F.

Storefront

Shop gate. Kiki runs out. She glances to the right
at the sidewalk, then runs diagonally across the
street. Kiki enters and diagonally crosses the
frame.

(S.E.) VRROOM VRRMM

Car passing with warning whistle. Kiki nervously
turns around in the middle of the street.

(S.E.) VRRRMMM

She dashes off as a truck skims past her.
Kiki runs to the sidewalk, then to the shop
window across the street. She quickly regains her
composure and casually walks O.O.F.
Kiki boldly marches forward. Jiji hisses.

JIJI: Kiki, in the city, you can't just run
out into the street.
KIKI: I'm sorry. We're still alive, aren't we?

She notices something. Chirpy city girls approach.

GIRLS A, B, C, D: Ha ha ha ha.
GIRL C: Look, you know how boys are.

Kiki walks on. She's completely self-conscious.
They approach and pass by each other.

GIRL A: He's so cute. I hope he's still invited
to her birthday party.
GIRL D: Don't you?
GIRL C: Yeah! (etc.)

Both O.O.F.
Kiki strides around the corner.

She looks pensive. Window reflects her and
building across the street.
Kiki glances at herself in the shop window.

KIKI: I wish I had something pretty to
wear. My dress is so ugly.

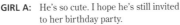

Supermarket Interior

Packed with merchandise. Kiki looks around as she
pushes her cart forward.
She examines a fry pan in the home appliance
section. She checks the price.

KIKI: Oh, wow! This costs so much!

Jiji finds a cat mug on the dining ware counter.
He shouts.

JIJI: Kiki, look! It's me!

A woman punching in prices. The mug is included.
Kiki looks at the cash register figures then at her
bills. She checks the register again.
She hands out several bills. The clerk's hand takes
them.
Kiki receives change and the receipt.

(S.E.) KLAK KLAKK CHING

Supermarket Entrance

Carrying two large bags, she backs into the door
and exits. She shifts her bags. The door closes
behind her.

JIJI: Any money left, Kiki?
KIKI: Not much. Looks like all we can
afford to eat now is pancakes.

Alley

Kiki carrying her shopping bags. She approaches
an old elegant boutique. Kiki stops. Jiji stops.

Kiki gazing at the display. She approaches the
window and stares at the enamel shoes inside.
CLOSE on enamel shoes. The shoes are on sale
but…

KIKI: They're so expensive!

Kiki stares at the display. Jiji walks up and leaps
onto the windowsill.
Further down the alley, a junk car filled with kids
rumbles toward them.

(S.E.) VROM PUFF PUFF KTHUNK

BOYS: Ha ha ha. Whoa! Hee hee hee.

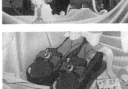

They're swaying. They're having fun. Tombo sees
Kiki. He leans forward and shouts.

TOMBO: Hey! Pull over!

Kiki standing in front of the shop. The junk car
enters from the front right and stops behind Kiki.

(S.E.) KREECH
BOOM!

TOMBO: Hey there! Miss Witch!

Kiki turns around. She can't turn too quickly
though because her arms are full.

KIKI: …!!

She's mortified.

The boys on the junk sports car. Tombo is waving
at her.

TOMBO: How come you're not flying today?

Kiki is infuriated.

KIKI: …!!

TOMBO: You can tell she's a witch 'cause she
always wears a dark dress.

He boasts to his friends while Kiki turns and walks
away to the left O.O.F. Tombo is alarmed by her
reaction.

TOMBO: Hey, wait! Come back, please. I didn't mean to insult you!

His friends burst into laughter.

BOYS: Yeah! Better luck next time, Tombo!

Kiki marches off O.O.F.

Bakery Courtyard

PAN DOWN from sky. Kiki is entering. Jiji by her feet. They pass by a three-wheeled truck. The door opens. Osono's face appears. Kiki stops.

OSONO: Oh, Kiki, perfect timing!

Kiki stares at her.

KIKI: Hmm…?!
OSONO: (O.O.F.) There's a lady here who wants you to make a delivery! She's your first customer.
KIKI: Customer! Oh, my. I'll be right back!

She looks surprised. She rushes upstairs to the right O.O.F.

Attic Room

Spruced up room. Sound of Kiki rushing upstairs.

(S.E.) THUMP THUMP

Jiji appears at the window. Kiki runs in and nearly trips over the raised floor.

KIKI: Oh.

She starts running, letting her bags topple from the table.

(S.E.) TUMP TUMP KRRSH

KIKI: Now, where's that map?

She rummages through her paper bag and retrieves a city map. She runs to the bed O.O.F.

Shop Interior

The yard door opens as light enters and Kiki leaps forward. She closes the door and runs to the shop. She enters the shop and suddenly stops. Her gaze moves from center right to front. A beautiful cosmopolitan woman regards Kiki. She seems friendly.

WOMAN: …
KIKI: …!!

Flustered, Kiki blushes.
Osono explains.

OSONO: Dear, this lady is a customer of ours, and we were talking about your new delivery service.

WOMAN: What a charming girl!

Kiki curtsies.

KIKI: My name's Kiki, ma'am.

WOMAN: Osono's told me great things about you. Do you think you can deliver this by tonight?

She indicates the covered birdcage. The cover has a slit.

KIKI: Yeah! I can.

Kiki smiles with an enthusiastic nod.
Inside the cage is a black cat holding a card in its mouth.

WOMAN: (O.O.F.) It's a birthday gift for my nephew. But something came up at work, and I can't make it to the party on time.

KIKI: I can get it there for you, guaranteed. Show me on the map where you want it delivered.

Jiji cautiously moves to the front left. He leaps O.O.F. and approaches the top of the cash register and peeks into the cage. It's a stuffed animal resembling Jiji. Jiji is astonished.

JIJI: Huh? But that's me.

He looks over to Kiki, but she and her client are looking over the open map.

WOMAN: Are you sure it won't be too far?
KIKI: I can fly there straight from here.

Woman looks at her.

WOMAN: Great, how much will it cost?

Kiki folds up the map.

KIKI: Oh. Well, I haven't really thought about a price.

Woman smiles and extends her right arm.

WOMAN: Aha! How about this much then?
KIKI: …

Her hand offered to Kiki. Kiki looks down at her hand and accepts the money. She gasps at the amount.

KIKI: This much for me? That's great! Thank you!

Backstreet

Tombo riding his bike.

Slope under the bakery. He passes under an overpass and comes forward. He brakes suddenly with a squeak.

(S.E.) KREECH

He backs up and looks up to the upper right. The cage hangs from Kiki's broom as she launches off the cliff. Tombo's thrilled at the sight!

TOMBO: Yeah! I gotta see this!

He steps off his bike, turning it around. He climbs the hill O.O.F. Kiki circles above.

Tombo pedals frantically up the bakery hill. Osono gazes up at the sky from the hilltop. Tombo rides onto the sidewalk.

(S.E.) KRRSH KRRSH KLANG

Next to Osono, he looks up at the sky.

TOMBO: She's the most amazing girl!
OSONO: She sure is!

Kiki circles up into the sky.

TOMBO: Hey, what can you tell me about her?

Tombo asks Osono. Osono turns around.

The Sky

Kiki winds up the sky. She fills up the frame as she ascends.
Kiki flies up in an arc pattern. She slows down near the end of the shot.

JIJI: Kiki, how high do you intend to go?
KIKI: This is my first job...

She takes out her map from under her dress, looks around and verifies the location.

KIKI: ...and I do not want to be stopped by that traffic cop.
JIJI: Hmm. Well, don't look now, but that's an airplane flying under us.

Jiji is curled up like a ball of string as he taunts her.
The plane passes under them.
The clipped map corresponding to the area down below.

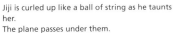

KIKI: Now, let's see. Yep! It's just past the cape.

She checks again and then puts the map away.

KIKI: Here we go!

She grabs her broom with both hands and ascends. She kicks out her legs and then free falls O.O.F.

JIJI: Whoa, boy!

Kiki falls toward the frame size bird's eye view of the neighboring district.
As soon as she's tiny she flies forward.
Kiki heads for a new town on the other side of the bridge. A seaplane flies under her.

Kiki speeding by. Her skirt and hair rustling in the wind. Kiki shouts.

KIKI: I'm getting to like this town more and more.
JIJI: I'm getting sick to my stomach.
KIKI: I can't wait to write Mom and Dad about my new business.

Above City

Kiki flies over group housing and suburban houses.
Ready-built houses and roads in the new housing development.
Kiki flies above.
Birds flying. More woods down below.
The flock approaches Kiki from behind. Kiki turns around. There's a sparkle in her eye.

KIKI: Wow! Look who's behind us. Wild geese!

Jiji looks. The birds fly over and past Kiki.

KIKI: And they're coming with us!

Kiki swerves a little and ascends.
The geese fly effortlessly. Kiki is right behind them. She flies up next to them.

The geese cry.

GEESE: KAHH KAHH KAHH

Kiki assumes they're welcoming her.

GEESE: KAHH KAHH KAHH

Continue PAN. The noisy geese. They're a little excited.

Kiki is puzzled.

KIKI: They seem awfully upset.
JIJI: They say they're going to fly higher.

Jiji appears to understand the geese calls.

KIKI: Huh?
JIJI: They say a gust of wind's coming.
KIKI: Oh!

She looks at the flock.
The right side of the flock. A sudden gust.

(S.E.) FWEEE

They roll over and rapidly ascend O.O.F.
A gust of wind comes in from the right side of the flock. The geese ride this wind upward in succession like dominos. Kiki is taken by surprise. The wind rushes in.

(S.E.) Sound of Wind

A gust hits Kiki.

KIKI: AIIEE.

She's swept by the wind. She's blown away. The geese continue their ascent.

She spins forward. The birdcage slips off her broom and falls. They're above a forest. The birdcage falls into the forest.
As she spins from the gust, she tries to steady her flight.

KIKI: Uh-ohhhh!!

Kiki can't afford to worry about how messy her skirt is. She dives down after the falling birdcage.

She catches up to the falling birdcage. She reaches for it, pulling it toward her. She tries to go back up while holding the cage, but falls instead. Trees enter from below as Kiki disappears.

(S.E.) FSSSHH

Inside the Forest

(S.E.) KAHH KAHH KAHH-

The jackdaw crow goes wild. It flaps its wings frantically up close.
Kiki caught on a tree branch.
She gapes at the frantic scene. She sees its nest.

(S.E.) KAHH KAHH

Crow nest with several eggs.

KIKI: Ahh! A nest!

Kiki finally understands the crow's panic. It lunges after her.

KIKI: Oh, I'm sorry! Ow! Oh!

(S.E.) KAHH KAHH KAHH

Hearing the warning call, other crows shoot up while Kiki tries to escape the crow as she escapes the trees.
Kiki profusely apologizes to the crow.

KIKI: I wasn't trying to steal your eggs! Really!

(S.E.) KAHH KAHH

The crow isn't so forgiving.
It squawks, quickly rolls over and flies to the right O.O.F.

Kiki watches it, then looks ahead.

KIKI: Oh, my goodness!

Kiki surprised.

JIJI: That was your fault. The geese were
kind enough to warn us of that wind.
But would you listen?

KIKI: Oh, be quiet!

Kiki calmly looks up at the geese.
The geese fly across in formation. Kiki looks up at
them, amazed at the sight.

KIKI: Look at them! Up so high. That gust
of wind took them all the way up.

Jiji shouts. Kiki turns.

JIJI: (O.O.F.) Kiki, we've got a problem!

KIKI: …?!

JIJI: The toy fell out!

Jiji shouts with the cage lid open. It only contains
the card.
Kiki stops suddenly and looks inside the cage.

KIKI: We've gotta go back!

She looks back, spinning in the air.

JIJI: Back to where?

KIKI: Where we fell!

She goes back.
Kiki rushes back O.O.F. to the front left. The forest
approaches. Suddenly…

(S.E.) KAHH KAHH KAHH

A flock of crows takes off.
Kiki panics.

KIKI: …!!

Crows warn her.

(S.E.) KAHH KAHH
(S.E.) KAHH KAHH

Crows multiply, swirling in the air. Kiki enters.

She hesitates, slows down, and circles.
She doesn't know what to do.

JIJI: They're calling you an egg stealer.
And you don't wanna know what
else. If I were you, I wouldn't go
back down there…again.

KIKI: We have to! Hold on!

(S.E.) KAHH KAHH

LONG SHOT. A crow suddenly emerges from the
forest.

It tries intimidating Kiki by grazing her face. Kiki is
caught off-guard.

KIKI: AIEEE!

Another crow attacks her.

KIKI: Oh.

She narrowly dodges them. Another bird. Three
birds now. An entire flock rushing up toward
her. Two, three birds, then a whole flock rushes
by O.O.F.

KIKI: AIEEE!

She can't fight back so she tries dodging them.
The flock of crows crosses over and flies upwards.
Kiki escapes.

(S.E.) KAHH KAHH KAHH

The crows attack her broom brush.
They bite her with every pass. Kiki is
overwhelmed.

KIKI: Oh, no! Kiki, brace yourself!

She's at her wit's end. She starts swinging the
birdcage.

KIKI: Leave us alone! Stop it!

Kiki enters from the lower right as she flies away
from the flock of crows. The crows eventually
stray off.
Kiki goes further left. The crows circle to the right.

Panorama of Forest

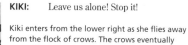

The dot-like crows still fly around in a frenzy.
Kiki enters near the front. She slowly comes to a
halt in midair. She's dumbfounded.

KIKI: Maybe we better rethink our plan.

JIJI: Frankly, I think this is a major insult.
Crows used to serve witches and do
what you told them.

KIKI: Hey, that was a long time ago, okay?

Kiki is indignant.

Jiji doesn't respond, but turns.

JIJI: How about if we go in after dark?

KIKI: We won't be able to make it in time.

Kiki in despair. She turns to the crows.

KIKI: …

She looks at Jiji with a determined face.

KIKI: Unless we buy ourselves some time.

Kiki Flying

Jiji shouts from inside the cage.

JIJI: You gotta be kidding!

KIKI: You can just pretend to be the doll
until I find the real one.

She zooms away.

House on Cliff/In the Sky

Cliff overlooking the sea. A single house standing
in the middle of a pasture in the sunset. A white
fence surrounds it. There are cows.
Kiki is nervous. Jiji looks at the house as they
approach it.

JIJI: Uh-oh!

KIKI: Don't worry. Hold still.

JIJI: Can I breathe?

KIKI: No! No breathing.

Bird's eye view of the house. Kiki enters from the
front right. She changes direction and descends.

House on Cliff/Door

Kiki lands by the open entrance. She hops off the
broom and walks up to the house.
She props the broom against her shoulder and
presses on the bell.

(S.E.) BRRING

She stands at the center nervously.
She waits a while. Then a boy comes rushing in.

BOY: It must be my present from Auntie!!

He runs, snatches the cage away, and lifts the
cover, revealing Jiji inside. He lifts the cage.

BOY: This is dumb!

He shakes the cage vigorously. Jiji wobbles, then falls over with a tap. Jiji frantically imitates a stuffed animal.

BOY: Ha ha ha.

The boy laughs. Kiki panics, but the boy runs back into the house.

KIKI: Uhm.

Mother shows up instead. Kiki nervous. Mother is outgoing.

MOTHER: You're a bit late! After my sister
           telephoned, we were wondering
           where you were.

KIKI: Uh, I'm sorry. Uh…

Suddenly recalling the procedure, she takes out her handbook.

KIKI: …

She snatches the pencil from the handbook. Her movements are clumsy because of the broom on her shoulder.
She opens up the handbook and offers it.

KIKI: Ah…Um. Could I please have your
           signature, ma'am?

Mother holds pencil, and quickly scribbles her signature on Kiki's handbook. Footsteps inside.

(S.E.) THUMP THUMP

Mother returns pencil and turns around. Kiki looks too. She responds before the mother.

BOY: (O.O.F.) Mom, can I put the canary
           in here?

MOTHER: Uh-huh.

The boy holds Jiji by his tail after taking him out of the cage.

MOTHER: (O.O.F.) But you be sure not to let
           it fly away, Ket.

BOY: 'Kay.

Fortunately, the boy only seems interested in the cage. He runs O.O.F.

Kiki panics. She glances at the mother then puts away the handbook. She steps back, declaring…

KIKI: Thank you! Enjoy your present!

She turns around and runs.
Kiki straddles the broom, runs and quickly ascends O.O.F. She flies up into the sky, then levels off and vanishes.

Mother steps out to have a look. She holds her waist as she admires the sight, whistling.

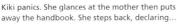

MOTHER: Well! Woo–

Jiji thrown onto the living carpet.
He bounces, then comes to a halt, and remains frozen.
A canary flaps its wings and the boy talks. Jiji glances over at them, his eyes wide open.

(S.E.) THUMP THUMP THUMP

BOY: Come on, you stupid bird!
(S.E.) THUMP THUMP

BOY: I got a brand new home for you.

He stands on the armrest with his hand inside the small birdcage. The boy tries to grab the frantic canary. PAN DOWN to an old dog napping on the carpet.

Jiji's in serious trouble. He whimpers.

JIJI: Please hurry, Kiki.

(S.E.) THUMP THUMP

Although the old dog is deaf to the commotion of the boy and bird, he catches an odd whiff. He sniffs, drowsily opens his eyes, and slowly blinks.

Inside the Forest

Forest bathed in western sunlight. The sky is still blue. Several crows above. PAN DOWN to the dark forest ground. Mossy stones, branches covered with ivy, small trees, and a toppled tree.

Kiki patiently searches the area. She runs up to a tree trunk. She scans through the branches.
The ground is covered with dry branches and pebbles.
She looks up a tree. The dense branches obstruct the view above. Crows fluttering.

(S.E.) KAHH KAHH

Kiki looks up.

KIKI: I know you fell close by, so you've
           got to be here somewhere.

She stares in, then walks left O.O.F.

Clearing in the Woods

Kiki walks into a clearing.
There seems to be something up ahead. She stops and looks.
It's a small log cabin in this isolated area. Branches block the view of the roof.
Kiki is intrigued.

KIKI: …!!

She dashes over to the cabin window.
The stuffed animal is sitting behind the window.
Kiki enters frame as she puts her left hand on the sill. She leaps and shouts. The glass turns transparent from her shadow.

KIKI: There you are!

She looks inside, jumps down, and moves left O.O.F.

Log Cabin Entrance

Terrace with entrance. The door and windows are open.
Kiki skips up to the terrace and calls inside.

KIKI: Hello! Anyone home?

She cautiously enters.

KIKI: Is anybody here? Anybody? Hello!

She calls and looks around.
The furnishings are spare. There's bread on the table and a jar of jam. It's cramped. A blank white canvas on an easel sits in the middle of the room.

Paintings propped against the wall. There's a cooking stove, clothes, bed cover, and paints sprawled all over the floor. A well-worn paintbox. Crusty paint on a palette.

The windowsill. A bottle of spirits and the cat doll. Kiki's eyes glued to the doll. She looks around again, and then calls before entering without permission.

KIKI: Anybody here?
URSULA: (O.O.F.) Yes! Stop shouting!

A young woman shouts from outside. Kiki is surprised. She steps back and looks around outside.

URSULA: I'm on the roof! What do you want?
           Why don't you come up?

179

She runs up to the ladder and looks up at the roof. She steps onto the ladder with the broom tucked under her arm as she climbs up.

Rooftop

Kiki climbs the ladder.

KIKI: ...!!

The rooftop surprises her. (TRACK BACK) There's her enemy, the crow.

CROW: KUHH.

It whimpers and turns right. It skips back to its flock on the roof ridge.
The painter is sketching the birds.

URSULA: What do you want?

Kiki nervously explains, lowering her voice.

KIKI: Oh, well, you have a black cat...in your cabin window, and, you see, it's mine and I need it back.

The woman concentrates on her sketch. She leans forward and addresses the crows.

URSULA: You're a good birdie, aren't you?

She moves her hand, then gazes at the birds. She's frank without being offensive.

URSULA: So, why was it alone in the forest, huh?

Kiki is drawn to her.

KIKI: That's where I dropped it. Um, may I have it back, please?
URSULA: I really need to finish this.

She turns to a fresh sheet.

URSULA: That's my girl!

She sits still and begins sketching. She seems to be comfortable with these birds.

Curious crows approach. The birds move.
Quick sketch motions. CLOSE on birds.

KIKI: ...

Kiki at a loss. She can't be any delayed anymore. But she doesn't want to be too forceful either. She glances up at the sky and then looks ahead.

Log Cabin Interior

Ursula enters the cabin. Sun going down.

URSULA: Well, why didn't you tell me sooner why you needed it in such a hurry?

Ursula goes O.O.F. behind the canvas. Kiki stands at the entrance.
Kiki watches, then looks up at her.
Ursula gives the black cat doll to Kiki.

URSULA: He keeps me company. I've gotten sort of fond of him, you know?

KIKI: Thank you.

Kiki suddenly notices.

KIKI: Oh!!

CLOSE on doll. Her right hand enters frame as she examines the torn and frayed neck. Cotton sticks out.

KIKI: His head's falling off.

Kiki is distressed. Ursula looks over.

URSULA: Ooh, it must have been the crows. They were making such a big fuss over him.

KIKI: This is terrible. I can't deliver it like this.

Kiki is overwhelmed. Ursula watches her, then makes a suggestion.

URSULA: Hmm. Hey! I know. How about we work out a deal?

Kiki is puzzled.

KIKI: Huh?!

Both (after pause)

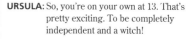

Kiki silently wiping the floor. Her skirt is soaked along with the floor.

URSULA: So, you're on your own at 13. That's pretty exciting. To be completely independent and a witch!

The interior of the room has grown dim. Kiki is wiping the floor.
Ursula outside the window. She looks in occasionally.

URSULA: Impressive!

Kiki continues wiping the floor.

KIKI: How's it going?
URSULA: Trust me. He'll be good as new.

On the terrace bench Ursula sews up the doll as she hums, surrounded by her paraphernalia brought outside. The sky is dimming.

The House on the Cliff/
Living Room

The living room where Jiji is held captive. The soft twilight comes through the window.

(S.E.) Sound of television

MOTHER: (O.O.F.) Ket, dear, turn off the TV!

Canary inside the cage. (PAN DOWN) The boy watching television. The old dog below.
Boy wears that typical child's "TV gaze." Jiji rests on his lap.

MOTHER: (O.O.F.) Your birthday guests are gonna be here soon! Ket, did you hear me?

He gets up slowly without replying. Jiji tips over on his side. Mother raises her voice.

MOTHER: Ket, turn off the TV!!

He stands upright suddenly and turns off the television.

(S.E.) KLIK

He runs off to the left O.O.F. His footsteps grow distant. Jiji is left alone with the old dog.
His eyes wide open, Jiji glances over at the old dog.
He's hoping the dog is asleep, but it turns to Jiji and drowsily opens its eyes. It wags its tail. Their eyes meet, but Jiji pretends to ignore him. He's breaking into a sweat.
The dog slowly rises and slumbers over to Jiji. Jiji's sweating won't stop.

The dog's muzzle enters the frame right in front of trembling Jiji on the brink of fainting. Jiji shuts his eyes.
The dog wriggles his nose, sticks its tongue out and licks Jiji.
The dog lazily raises its head, slowly circles the frozen Jiji, and then comes to a rest. His eyes closed, he's curled up around Jiji as if protecting him.
He lets out a sigh.
Jiji bug-eyed.

Cabin/Terrace

Sunset sky. Orange vanishing from the sky. A crow is exhausted from playing.
Ursula finishes up her sewing. The interior lights up with a glow. Ursula shouts.

URSULA: I'm done!

Kiki runs out, holding a lamp.

KIKI: Thank you very much!

Ursula stands and gives the doll to Kiki.

URSULA: Better go get Jiji before it's too late.

Kiki looks at the doll, then up at Ursula.

KIKI: But I haven't finished yet.

Ursula takes the lamp in Kiki's right hand (as Kiki replies).

URSULA: Don't worry. You've done enough.
             Now, go on and get him!
KIKI: Thanks!

Kiki runs from the front left as she thanks her and quickly straddles her broom. She gravitates upward and flies away at full speed over the trees.

Ursula watches her with a smile.

URSULA: Hmm.

House on Cliff/Exterior

It's nighttime. The entrance light glows. There are two more cars.

House on Cliff/Dining Room

Ket dining with his grandparents. A merry atmosphere with everyone laughing.

KET: (O.O.F.) Jeff likes my present more than me!

EVERYONE: Ha ha ha ha…

House on Cliff/Kitchen

House on Cliff/Dining Room

The old dog is lying down. Jiji is slightly visible. The conversation is lively. The sound of dining.

MOTHER: (O.O.F.) Jeff's such a funny dog.
             He simply adores that stuffed cat. He
             won't leave it alone!

FATHER: (O.O.F.) I'll bet he thinks it's a
             puppy!
GRANDMOTHER: (O.O.F.) He'll be upset
             when Ket wants to take it and play
             with it.

EVERYONE: (O.O.F.) Ha ha ha ha.
KET: (O.O.F.) That's okay. He can have it.

The old dog lifts its head and sniffs.

House on Cliff/Entrance Hall

The old dog enters, holding Jiji in his mouth.

GRANDMOTHER: (O.O.F.) He's getting to be
             such an old dog.
KET: Yeah. All he does is sleep all day.
FATHER: All day!

Jeff walks up to the door and paws the door.

(S.E.) KRIK KRIK

MOTHER: Ket, dear, go open the door. Jeff
             wants to go out.

Ket scuttles off chair.

(S.E.) KLAK KLAK

House on Cliff/Exterior

Entrance door. (laughter leaks through)
Ket and Jeff can be seen on the inside.

KET: Jeff, shut the door when you're
             done. Okay?

Jeff lumbers out. Ket recedes O.O.F. to the left. Gravel by the entrance. Old dog Jeff enters frame from the left.
He drops Jiji. Jiji lands on the ground and runs O.O.F. to the right.
Kiki runs out from behind the car.

KIKI: Jiji!!

She enters frame. Jiji leaps up and Kiki hugs him.

JIJI: What took you so long?
KIKI: I'm sorry!

Jiji sits up and points to Jeff.

JIJI: My friend, Jeff, helped me escape.

Kiki looks over.

KIKI: …

Jeff sits still. He wags his tail only once.

A dog rescuing a cat? Kiki is astonished.

JIJI: Kiki, if we ask him, I bet he'll take
             the stuffed one back inside.
KIKI: …

-pause-

Kiki stands up and walks to the front left O.O.F. She cautiously enters the frame, facing Jeff.

KIKI: Could you take this in, please?

Kiki gently offers the doll. Jeff softly bites it, stands up stoically, and then walks back to the left O.O.F. Kiki's point of view. Jeff lumbers back to the house. He enters through the open door, gently presses the door forward and closes it. A pause after it shuts.

Sky Above City

It's nighttime below. House lights flicker. Car lights winding down the roads.

Back shot of Kiki flying. The sea of lights in the city approaches in front.

Jiji stretching his neck. Kiki watches him.

KIKI: How are ya? Hungry?
JIJI: No, I'm tired!

KIKI: Yeah, me too. I'm very tired. We're
             both gonna sleep well tonight! By
             the way, that painter who found the
             stuffed cat told me she wants to do a
             drawing with me in it.

JIJI: Naked?
KIKI: Jiji!

The conversation concludes pleasantly. Kiki looks content.

Bakery

The store is still illuminated. Wreath bread hanging in the middle of the shop window. The husband is rushing back and forth.

CLOSE on the wreath bread. An elegant sign made of bread. (TRACK BACK) The husband walks back and forth inside.

HUSBAND: …!!

He notices something. Surprised, he looks out and up. He rushes to the back left. Osono looks up from her newspaper and watches her husband. As she looks to the front right she puts down her paper. Kiki descends in front of the shop window.

Kiki notices the wreath bread. She rushes forward, dazzled by the sight and reads the writing on the wreath. Jiji enters from below.
Kiki looks inside then rushes to the left. Kiki pushes the door open and runs into the store. Osono stands up.

She rushes to Osono as if shouting, "Is that…?!" The husband enters from back. Osono points at him. Kiki drops her broom and gives him a big hug. Osono bursts out laughing. FADE OUT.

Noon in the City

Clear blue sky. Shopping district is bustling.

(S.E.) bustle

Pedestrians crossing the street. People eating out.

From the bustle to the back streets.

Bakery

Kiki looking after the shop. The bakery street. Kiki is bored.

(S.E.) VRRROOM

Kiki notices something.
A boy's parked motorcycle. A girl runs toward it. They ride it together.

(S.E.) VRRRMMM

Kiki watches. She sighs.

KIKI: Hmmm.

The shop is quiet.

KIKI: Boring.
JIJI: Hey!

Jiji looks up at Kiki. He skips toward her. Kiki's slumped over.

JIJI: Wake up! You're supposed to be minding the store!

Kiki barely responds.

KIKI: I am, but today this place is boring.

Jiji glances outside.

JIJI: But it always gets busy about this time.

KIKI: I know that. That's not what I mean.

She looks at Jiji.

KIKI: I mean, my customers. Jiji, if nobody comes in, I'm gonna have to eat pancakes forever and be fat, fat, fat! And what am I supposed to do about that?

JIJI: Well, I like pancakes, provided they're not burned.

He doesn't understand Kiki's troubles. Kiki is disappointed. She mocks him.

KIKI: Look, fur ball, when you get as fat and round as a pancake, you see if I care.

Kiki sits upright.

(S.E.) TAK TAK TAK

The woman who sent the stuffed animal passes by quickly.
Kiki looks on smiling. The footsteps recede. Kiki looks serious.

KIKI: Beautiful, isn't she? They tell me she's a clothes designer.

She sighs deeply and leans against the counter.

JIJI: Her designs may be fabulous, but her cat's still a snob.

The cat has his own world.
The phone suddenly rings.

(S.E.) BRRING

Kiki stands up.

KIKI: Hello! Good Cooking Pan Bakery.

Kiki answers the phone enthusiastically. Then she raises her voice.

KIKI: What? Pardon? Uh, yes, ma'am.

Kiki cups the receiver with her hand.

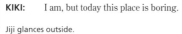

KIKI: 'Bout time we got a customer, huh? Uh, yes, ma'am, 4:30 will be a perfect time to pick it up.

Night and day difference in her attitude. Jiji is exasperated.

Storefront

Tombo looks in through the storefront window. He checks to see if Kiki is in, then moves O.O.F.

Store Interior

KIKI: Uh-huh. And the address? Yes. The blue roof. Right. Yeah. I'm pretty sure I have it all.

Kiki taking notes.

KIKI: And thank you very much, ma'am.

(S.E.) KLIK

The door opens. As she hangs up the phone she looks over, surprised.

TOMBO: Hi!

Tombo waves cheerfully as he approaches her without any malice. Kiki is annoyed. She looks away in disgust.

KIKI: Hmph!!

She still looks away.
Tombo stands in front of the counter. Jiji looks around and then exits.
Kiki stares at the right side of the map.

Kiki has hostile attitude.

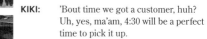

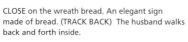

TOMBO: (O.O.F.) I'll take this, please.

He grabs a cookie and offers money. Kiki takes it. She opens the cash drawer with her left hand.

(S.E.) CHING CHIING

She gives him his change.

KIKI: Thank you very much. Good afternoon.

She opens up her map again.
Tombo is persistent.

TOMBO: Aw, come on. You're not still mad at me, are you? Listen. We're gonna have a huge party at the club tonight.

Kiki pretends to ignore him.

TOMBO: (O.O.F.) It's called the Aviation Club. And we'd really like for you to come. Here's your invitation.

Tombo's hand enters frame. Kiki can't resist glancing at it. A ribboned envelope. Kiki is nervous.

KIKI: …

TOMBO: It's a serious club for kids who are into flying and aircraft and stuff.

She glances up at him. He's unexpectedly being a gentleman.

TOMBO: And you know everybody would be really excited if you came.

Customer enters. Kiki gives a stilted response.

KIKI: Yes. May I help you, sir?
MAN: They tell me you have a delivery service.

Kiki is surprised.

KIKI: Oh…Oh, I'm sorry. Yes, of course, we can handle it.
MAN: It's very urgent that this package arrive as soon as possible.
KIKI: That's no problem.

She takes the package, but then puts it down.

KIKI: Oh!!

(S.E.) THUDD

MAN: Uh, are you all right?
KIKI: Uh-huh.

She staggers as she moves it.

TOMBO: Can I help you?
KIKI: Uh. Ohhh…

She takes it to the scale. It lands with a thud.

She examines the needle. She holds it steady, stands and goes to the back right. She starts taking notes.

TOMBO: Well, I hope you make up your mind by 6 o'clock, 'cause that's when I'll be by to pick ya up. See ya!

Tombo rushes O.O.F.

KIKI: Uh-ah…

Kiki tries to stop him.

MAN: How much will that be?

KIKI: Will that be inside or outside city limits, sir?

Kiki flustered. She glances over at the exit where Tombo exited.

MAN: I wrote the address on the box!

Kiki finally notices and exclaims.

KIKI: Oh-oh, the box! Oh, I'm sorry.

Kitchen

Osono is knitting.
Footsteps running upstairs.

(S.E.) THUMP THUMP

Kiki rushes into the kitchen.

(S.E.) THUMP THUMP

She nearly runs into the wall and turns to the front left.

KIKI: Osono! Osono!

She runs up to Osono.

KIKI: I've got a big problem! I got an invitation to go to a party at Tombo's flying club!

Osono remains calm.

OSONO: I'm sure it'll be a great party, Kiki.
KIKI: No! But my problem is, what am I going to wear?

It turns out she really wants to go.
Osono understands. She looks her over. Then she teases her.

OSONO: Kiki, you haven't got a problem. You look fine in that. Besides, it makes you look beautiful and mysterious.

Kiki sounds serious.
KIKI: Really?
OSONO: How's work?

She suddenly remembers her assignments and looks at her watch.

KIKI: I almost forgot about that! It's already 4 o'clock! Oh, no!

She rushes to the right and exits the room. Her face pokes out.

KIKI: Can you watch the store until I get back, Osono?

She rushes O.O.F.

KIKI: (O.O.F.) Jiji? Jiji?
OSONO: HMMM…

Osono chuckles at the sight.

City Sky

Kiki flies over the roofs. The package is too heavy. Kiki descends. She sways toward a dome, ricochets off it, and flies diagonally to the front.

Kiki skims over the roofs.

JIJI: You were so mad at that boy. I don't understand why you're going to his party.

KIKI: Please don't talk. I'm tryin' to fly this broom, okay?

Kiki flies over the city. She crosses over a city gas lamp.

Apartment Stairs

She takes the package up, step by step. She hoists it onto the landing. She's panting as she hoists it up again.

Apartment Hall

KIKI: Thank you very much.

She shuts and then runs to the front.

JIJI: Come on, Jiji!

City Sky

Clock tower in the distance. Kiki soars through.

KIKI: We can't keep our next appointment waiting.

Bay

Kiki whizzes by.

Residential Road

Kiki arrives and stops in front of a mansion gate.

KIKI: There's the blue roof!!

She descends and flies up to above the stairs.

Old Mansion

She descends onto the porch. Kiki stands in front of the door. Jiji leaps to the ground. Kiki taps the doorknocker.

(S.E.) TOK TOK

She releases the doorknocker.

The door quietly opens.

(S.E.) KLIK

An old woman emerges.

KIKI: …My name's Kiki, and someone telephoned for a delivery service, so here I am.

BARSA: Right this way, dear.

Kiki walks forward and enters. The door closes.

(S.E.) KLIK

Inside the Mansion

The luxurious interior looks worn. Kiki follows the old maid, Barsa.

BARSA: You are right on time.
KIKI: Thank you.

Bright room seen from the spare room.

BARSA: Oh, madam, the delivery girl is here.

Kitchen

A large, bright kitchen.

OLD LADY: My, delivery time already?

She looks at Kiki.

OLD LADY: Come in, dear. Please make yourself right at home.

BARSA: (to Kiki) Please do.
KIKI: Thanks.

Barsa turns to Kiki.

BARSA: May I take that for you?

Kiki moves to front right. Barsa notices something.

BARSA: …?!

Jiji walks as if hiding under Kiki's skirt.
Barsa says to herself.

BARSA: Broom and a black cat. Well, it's just as my great-grandmother told me.

Kiki stops. She introduces herself.

KIKI: My name's Kiki, and I'm a witch.
BARSA: Mm-hmm. Oh, my, what a pretty witch you are.

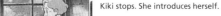

BARSA: I'm so sorry, but that special treat you were supposed to deliver…isn't ready yet.

She turns the dial.

BARSA: I think there's something wrong with it. It's got a mind of its own, and it doesn't want to heat up.

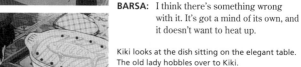

Kiki looks at the dish sitting on the elegant table. The old lady hobbles over to Kiki.

OLD LADY: It's old. Like me, it's seen better days. I was hoping you'd be able to deliver a dish to my granddaughter's birthday party. It's my specialty: herring and pumpkin potpie.

She looks at the oven then at Kiki.

OLD LADY: But I must admit defeat.

The brightness contrasts against her solitude.

OLD LADY: I'll have to phone her and tell her I'm sorry. I feel just awful having you come here for nothing. Barsa!

She calls on Barsa at the entrance.

OLD LADY: (O.O.F.) Barsa!

Barsa is straddling the broom.

OLD LADY: (O.O.F.) Would you get Kiki's money, please?

BARSA: Certainly, madam.
OLD LADY: All of it. Pay her what we agreed on.
KIKI: …!!

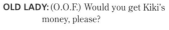

Kiki turns, surprised.

KIKI: Oh, no, I couldn't!
OLD LADY: Please accept it. This was all my fault.

Kiki hesitates. Then her face lights up.

KIKI: Ma'am, since I don't have any other jobs, maybe I can help. How about we use that old oven over there?

She looks over at the oven behind the old lady, who's puzzled.

OLD LADY: Hmm…? Well, maybe?

She looks back at Kiki.

OLD LADY: It used to bake beautiful bread, but I haven't baked in it lately.

KIKI: Well, if it burns firewood, I can help you. I used to help my mom bake all the time.

The lady hesitates.

OLD LADY: But it's such a big job to build a fire.
BARSA: A great idea, ma'am. I never liked that electric thing. I think her plan is perfect.

Kiki insisting.

KIKI: Ma'am, it'll work, really.
OLD LADY: You think so?

She hesitates, but then exclaims.

OLD LADY: All right then. Let's try it!!

Mansion Yard

Firewood shack. Kiki opens the door and enters. Kiki grabs several heavy logs and tucks them under her arm.

JIJI: Don't blame me if you're late for your party.

KIKI: I can't take her money and not help out.

Kiki runs out. She shuts the door with her back and runs to the front right.

KIKI: Okay, Jiji, let's go.

Kitchen

The maid enters the frame, pumping the windbag.

BARSA: Madam, here. Look what I found.

Kiki takes out a match, strikes it to ignite the pile of firewood.

OLD LADY: You're a very clever girl, my dear. Your mother must be proud.

Wood and paper. Kiki pulls her hand back and watches the flame.
The flame spreads.
The lady presses her hand against her chest.

OLD LADY: Oh, well, this is exciting.

BARSA: Mm-hmm. Yes, this is much better.

Chimney smoke. The firewood burns.
Kiki wipes her brow.

KIKI: Hoof.

Large clock.
She pushes back the wood with a poker.

OLD LADY: It should be about time.

Kiki puts down the poker and puts the dish into the furnace.
Kiki's hand slides it in. She quickly grabs the lid.
Latches it shut.

(S.E.) KLANG

She backs out and skips down.

OLD LADY: Now we wait.
KIKI: You think 40 minutes should be about right?
OLD LADY: Exactly right. So why don't we take a little break?

KIKI: Maybe I can help around the house while the pie is baking.

Jiji listens. He's worried about the time.

OLD LADY: Oh, how nice of you to offer.

Mansion/Entrance Hall

Barsa looks up.

BARSA: What a wonderful witch.
KIKI: There we go.

Kiki changes the light. Jiji is muttering.

JIJI: You're never gonna make the party on time.

Kiki sticks out the bulb. Jiji grabs it with his mouth.

KIKI: Stop worrying. It'll only take me 15 minutes if I fly there fast.

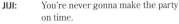
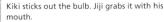

The old lady looks in.

OLD LADY: Would you like some hot tea? It's no trouble.

Kitchen

Kiki and the old lady having tea.

OLD LADY: …!! Dear. What did you say to me was the time of your party?

KIKI: It's at 6 o'clock, but it's only 15 minutes away.

The clock.
Old lady raises her voice.

OLD LADY: Oh, my goodness. I'm afraid my clock runs about 10 minutes slow.

Kiki panics. She stands up.

KIKI: I'm gonna be late!

OLD LADY: Check the potpie and see if it's ready.
KIKI: Oh!

Kiki runs. The old lady strains to get up.

OLD LADY: Help! Barsa, come!

Kiki runs, wears the potholders, unlatches the oven, and looks in. She slides her hands in and pulls out the dish with both hands.

KIKI: Is the pie baked? Is it ready?

Lady examines it. The maid enters the frame.

OLD LADY: It seems fine. Now, you'd better hurry.
KIKI: Uh-huh.

She puts the potpie into the basket. She lowers the dish and puts a potholder under the basket handle to lower the dish. Barsa's hand puts the lid on the dish.

Hall

Barsa runs out. She returns the broom. She shouts into the kitchen.

BARSA: I got the broom. We're ready! Come on!

Kitchen

KIKI: Okay!

She's about to take off when the lady presses money into her left hand.

OLD LADY: Let me pay you for your time.

Kiki's taken aback.

KIKI: But that's much too much!!

OLD LADY: Not for all of your help.

The lady smiles. The maid returns.

BARSA: Hurry up.

Kiki curtsies.

Barsa gives her broom.

BARSA: Hurry up!

Kiki runs to the back exit. The maid runs after her.

Sky Above the Mansion

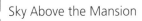

Kiki ascends as she finds her direction. Stormy winds. The light flashes.
The wind howls. Kiki flying.

KIKI: We can beat the rain if we just fly a little faster.

JIJI: Not according to my whiskers.

The sky turns dark. It starts to rain, and then it pours. Cityscape of rain.

Kitchen

Behind the window. The maid comes up next to the lady looking up. They look at each other. The rain is relentless. Water is pouring off the roof.

(S.E.) FSSSHHH

They look outside, worried about Kiki.

City Sky

Kiki flying with the basket tucked underneath her skirt.
She is drenched in the storming rain.
Kiki's hair and clothes sag completely. Her face is drenched, too.

JIJI: Could we get out of the rain, please? I'm begging you!
KIKI: We can't! That'll make us even later, and the food will get cold if we stop.

They fly to the wealthy district.

Bakery Hill

Tombo walks up the rainy slope. He's wearing a suit.
He looks inside the bakery. After a pause he comes out and looks around. He runs out under the awning, glances up at the sky, and then checks his wristwatch.

(S.E.) BONG BONG

Clock tower chimes at 6 o'clock.
The sky is very dark.

Granddaughter's House

The entrance of a new residential district surrounded by expensive cars. The house is illuminated.
Kiki enters the frame from the front right. She descends in front of the entrance beyond the cars. Kiki lands. She hugs the basket, and gets off her broom. She scuttles over to the entrance, clumsily holding up her skirt.

Granddaughter's House/Entrance

A gaudy colonial design entrance.
Kiki enters the terrace hall and puts the basket on the floor. Jiji also leaps down.

She carries the basket as she approaches the door. She shifts the broom in her left hand and rings the bell. She steps back and glances inside the basket. She rubs her left hand against something as if it's too wet, then combs the front of her soaked hair. The door opens.

(S.E.) KLIK

Kiki stands upright.

The door opens. A dressed up girl smiles (she thinks it's her guest). She suddenly turns cold when she sees Kiki. She sizes her up arrogantly and then hisses.

GIRL: Yes? What do you want?
KIKI: I have a delivery.

Kiki puts on a smile and offers the basket. The girl looks at it.

GIRL: But it is soaking wet.

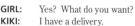

Kiki's surprised by the contrast between her and her grandmother, but she glances down at the basket and explains.

KIKI: Oh, well, I'm sorry. It began to rain on the way. But don't worry. The food came through all right.

The girl's voice enters frame while Kiki explains as it seizes the basket from Kiki.
She pulls it back and looks in. She's dismayed.

GIRL: Oh, no, I told Grandma I didn't want that.

MOTHER: (O.O.F.) Hey, what'd you get?
GIRL: Oh, Grandma sent me another one of her crummy herring pies again.

The girl directs her voice inside. Kiki takes out her handbook and pencil.

KIKI: Um, will you please sign this receipt for me?
GIRL: I hate Grandma's stupid pies.

She grabs the pencil, quickly scribbles her signature. She slaps the pencil onto the handbook, steps back and shuts the door on Kiki's face.

(S.E.) CHUD

The party noise fades out with the sound of rain. Kiki stands still, taken aback.

KIKI: …

Jiji, by her feet, is furious.

JIJI: I cannot believe they're related.

Blows raspberry.

Water still drips off her skirt.
She turns around and walks away. Jiji follows. They leave the puddle behind.

Granddaughter's House/ Long Shot

Kiki flies to the front from the entrance.
Kiki coasts through the rain. The rain drenches her. Water flowing down her face.
Jiji shouts from behind.

JIJI: Maybe we still have time.

KIKI: …

She looks too upset to answer.

Bakery

Tombo's wrist. He pulls back his sleeve to look at his watch. It's very dark. The only light comes from the store.
The rain won't stop. Tombo looks up and takes a deep sigh.
The door opens and the husband appears. Their eyes meet.

They look up at the sky.
Tombo opens up his umbrella. He walks away. The husband looks on.

City Sky

Kiki flies above the illuminated neighborhood. The environment is cold and gray.
Every part of Kiki, her hair, her ribbon, etc., is drenched. Jiji looks over her shoulder and shouts.

JIJI: Kiki, there he is!

Kiki still looks upset.
Tombo's umbrella as he walks away. Kiki enters frame from the left.
She passes the courtyard. Jiji shouts.

JIJI: Come on! We can catch him!
Kiki doesn't respond.

Bakery/Kitchen

Osono behind the window in the lit up kitchen. She seems to be cooking. She notices something and looks at the window and opens it up.

Bakery/Courtyard

Osono calls on Kiki as she comes upstairs. Kiki stops and turns.

OSONO: Kiki? We were all so worried about you. And that poor boy waited such a long time.

Kiki in the rain. She's drenched. She has a half-transparent look, almost as if she's smiling.

KIKI: It doesn't matter anyway. I can't go in these wet clothes.

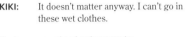

She turns around and rushes upstairs. The door opens and shuts.

(S.E.) CLATCH

Attic Room

Flower pot in the rain. Leaves flutter with raindrops.
The electric lamp on Kiki's clothes hanging on a string. They drip.

PAN DOWN to Kiki snuggled under the blanket. Jiji is beside her.

JIJI: Kiki, what's wrong? Are you not feeling well?
KIKI: …

She only shifts her position.
Kiki still snuggled under the blanket. Jiji is hungry though.

JIJI: Maybe we should eat something, okay?
KIKI: You eat.

Her right hand emerges from under blanket. Jiji looks.
There are bread slices in the breadbasket on the table.
The room has more everyday items, but it still looks desolate.

Kiki's hand draws back her hand. She's snuggled up again. Jiji jumps off the bed and onto the table. He chews on the bread.

Courtyard/Next Morning

FADE IN
The morning light shines on Kiki's room.

(S.E.) Birds chirping.

The window is damp. The curtains are drawn. The sky is pale blue.

Osono comes out and closes the door behind her. She's below Kiki's room and shouts.

OSONO: Kiki–

The windowsill rattles. Jiji's voice.

JIJI: Meow–

Jiji is scratching the windowsill from the inside.

(S.E.) SKRRCH SKRRCH SKRRCH

The curtains and sash shake a little.

OSONO: …?

Osono gazes up with a puzzled look. She walks up to the stairs.

Attic Room

Dim room. Jiji walks in from the right and waits by the door. Someone knocks on the door.

(S.E.) TOK TOK

JIJI: MEOW–

Jiji meows and runs right O.O.F. Osono looks on.

Jiji runs under the bed, turns toward her and cries. Kiki burrowed under the blanket.
Osono enters frame and approaches the bed.

OSONO: Not feeling very well, huh?

Kiki uncovers her face. Her hair is messy.
Osono touches Kiki's neck with her left hand. She's surprised.

OSONO: You have quite a fever.
KIKI: Uh-huh. My head's hurting so much.

Kiki's voice sounds awful.

OSONO: Well, you flew in that weather and you never really dried off.

Kiki's full of self-pity. She looks up miserably, her eyes opening up.

KIKI: Do you think I'm going to die, Osono?
OSONO: Huh?

Osono is speechless. Then she bursts out laughing.

OSONO: No, you're not. I'll bring some medicine right up...and maybe you should have some potpie.

Osono can tell Kiki's suffering from something besides a cold.
Kiki is a little upset by her laughter.

KIKI: Not that.

Osono understands.
She addresses both Kiki and Jiji.

OSONO: Well, then, I'll just make something else for you. How about some nice hot oatmeal with honey in it? You want some too?

Jiji's eyes light up. He says thank you!

JIJI: Meow–

Attic Room/(a little while later)

The pot of oatmeal is steaming. A large spoon scoops some out O.O.F.

OSONO: This oatmeal will pick ya right up.

Osono serves the oatmeal on the table now by Kiki's bedside. Osono crouches and puts a bowl on the floor.

OSONO: There ya go. Here. (She blows on it) Oof! Now, don't burn your tongue.

Osono stands and Jiji leaps onto the floor. She picks up Kiki's bowl and scoops out a spoonful of oatmeal. Jiji tiptoes up to the bowl and licks the oatmeal. He leaps up.

JIJI: Ow!

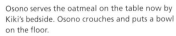

Osono puts the lid back on the pot and offers the bowl.

OSONO: You should come and eat your meal while it's still warm.

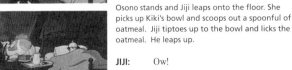

Kiki squirms under the blanket.

KIKI: Do I have to eat it?
OSONO: Only if you want to get well.

Osono leans over.

OSONO: Oh! You know that boy stopped by to see you again today.
KIKI: Huh?!

Kiki is speechless. Osono teases her.

OSONO: That's right. When I told him you were sick he asked me how a witch could catch cold in the first place… ha ha ha…
KIKI: …

Kiki's eyes, wide open.

OSONO: Oh, and he said he wanted to visit you a little later.

Kiki panics. She hides her face.

KIKI: Oh, my gosh! No!

OSONO: Well, I thought you might feel that way, so I turned him down politely. You must be tired. You try to get some sleep.

On her way to the door she opens up the window.

OSONO: Now, I'll just open up the window so you'll have some fresh air.

Kiki watches Osono. She pulls off her blanket slightly.

Kiki calls after Osono as she exits.

KIKI: (O.O.F.) Osono!
OSONO: Hmm?

Osono stops and turns around.

-pause-

Kiki shakes her head.

KIKI: Um, never mind.

Osono smiles and exits.
Sound of Osono descending stairs.

(S.E.) TUMP TUMP TUMP TUMP…

A while later.
It's quiet. Kiki looks across room, but then she returns her gaze and sighs.

KIKI: HOOF.

She's lonely.

Courtyard

Sunny yard. Kiki's clothes and ribbon are flapping in the wind. The sound of the city.

(S.E.) Traffic noise, voices, birds chirping, etc.

Attic Room

Morning. Kiki baking pancakes on the stove. She turns them over. The flame is weak. She examines the stove, pokes at it with her spatula. Smoke and sparks shoot out. She covers the flame with her pan, squints her eyes, and shouts.

KIKI: Jiji–

Courtyard

Jiji preens himself on the yard wall.

KIKI: (O.O.F.) Jiji–

JIJI: What? Hmm?

Jiji replies, but then stops. He looks to his right and stares.
Jiji's P.O.V. The stuck-up cat climbs onto his wall from the lower wall. She sits and preens herself.

Jiji freezes up.

JIJI: Hmm–

Jiji realizes how cute she is!! She licks her feet, looks up and finally notices Jiji. At least, that's how it looks to him.

LILY: Hmm?

Jiji is charmed by her blushing.
She thrills Jiji.

JIJI: Wow!

They stare at each other.

After a while, Jiji stands up and cautiously approaches her.

Room Window

Kiki calls out from the window for Jiji.

KIKI: Where are you?
OSONO: (O.O.F.) Kiki?

Kiki looks down. Osono looks up from the bakery door.

OSONO: Are you feeling better?
KIKI: A lot better. Thank you. I'm sorry, I didn't realize I'd overslept.
OSONO: That's okay. Come down later. I have a favor to ask you. All right?

KIKI: Okay.

Inside Bakery

Kiki takes the small package, then reads the writing.

KIKI: The name is "Koppori"?
OSONO: (offers money) Uh-huh. Now, take this money.

KIKI: (shakes her head) Oh, no, ma'am. No money. It's on me.

Osono smiles.

OSONO: Impossible. Work is work, and make sure you deliver it in person.

Osono puts the coins in her hand and winks at her strangely.

Courtyard

Kiki walks out, closes the door and calls out as she looks around.

KIKI: Jiji!

Jiji looks out from the roof. Lily also looks out.

JIJI: What is it?

Surprised, Kiki leans over and looks up.

KIKI: We've got a delivery. Hey, who's your friend there?

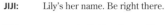

JIJI: Lily's her name. Be right there.

Jiji is so nervous maybe he'd prefer working. Kiki isn't foolish enough to stop someone's romance…

KIKI: Stay there. I'll be right back. He's all yours. Bye-bye.
LILY: Meow.

Lily meows back. Jiji looks embarrassed next to her.
Kiki smiles and walks to the right O.O.F.

Hill Road

Kiki descends the slope. She's beaming as she marches forward.

A coupe rumbles upward.

Alley

Kiki descends the hill, walking in the alley shade. A back alley. Then she passes a red roof and bright green yard beyond the alley's shaded stone walls and short stairs. She's impressed by the sight, but descends to the right O.O.F.

Narrow alley. It opens up beyond to a dazzling sight. Kiki emerges from the side streets, examines the note, and then walks to the bright area.

Terrace Overlooking the Sea

Kiki comes out onto a small terrace. The sea breeze puffs up her skirt.

KIKI: …! Wow…

Spellbound, she walks up to the edge.
The sea is right below. (PAN) Boats beached with the receding tide. Seagulls fly by.

She leans on the grating and gazes at the sight.

KIKI: It's so pretty...and warm.

Seagulls fly by. She nearly forgets her assignment.

Suddenly, Tombo emerges from beyond the wall. Was he inspecting the wind meter? Then he notices something.

TOMBO: Mmm!

TRACK BACK while Tombo leans forward. Kiki looking incredibly content. She doesn't even hear Tombo calling. He's now leaning over the wall, shouting.

TOMBO: Hey. Hey there, Miss Witch!
KIKI: …!!

She turns around. She's surprised to see Tombo.

KIKI: Huh?

Tombo smiles at her cordially.

TOMBO: Takin' a walk?

Kiki nervous. She vigorously shakes her head.

KIKI: Uh-uh. I'm looking for someone named, uh, Koppori.

Tombo reacts.

TOMBO: Hey, that's my name. That's me.

KIKI: Huh?!

She's speechless. Tombo points to the bottom left.

TOMBO: If you go around that way, I'll be right with you, okay?

He leaps behind the wall.
Kiki is bewildered. She has no idea what's going on.
She looks down at the package.

KIKI: Osono, how could you do this to me?

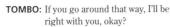

She finally realizes Osono's plan.

Tombo's House/Yard

Platform overlooking the sea. Lawn with flowers including orchids.
Tombo darts in from the right, waiting for Kiki at the gate. Kiki almost simultaneously descends the stairs. She gives the package to Tombo.

TOMBO: Gee, thanks a lot.

He leans against the gate column and opens it up, rummaging through it. He retrieves the note. He reads it. Kiki hesitates, but then speaks up.

KIKI: Um, about the other night? I'm sorry I didn't show up.
TOMBO: Huh? Mmm. I'm sorry you had to end up so sick like that.

He smiles pleasantly and puts the note into his pocket. A plane flies behind them.
Tombo then invites.

TOMBO: Hey, come over to my place. There's somethin' I wanna show ya.

Without waiting, he goes to the garden O.O.F.
Kiki steps to the right watching him, then hesitates.
Tombo turns around, inviting her.

TOMBO: Oh, you gotta see it.

The stairs apparently to the garden below.

Tombo's House/Garage

Dark garage interior. A bicycle equipped with a propeller.
(S.E.) KLAK KLAK

Tombo's hand lifts up the garage door. Kiki wonders what this is. Tombo smiles at her proudly. He marches forward.

TOMBO: The party was to celebrate the completion of this thing.

The bicycle. Tools scattered all over the floor. Further back, there's a dusty Model T Ford. Tombo enters frame from the front left.

TOMBO: This is the engine of a man-propelled plane.

He straddles the bicycle and begins pedaling.

TOMBO: Watch this.

The propeller begins spinning.

TOMBO: We're going to assemble the wings and the frame at somebody else's house.

The propeller continues spinning. Tombo proudly pedals away.

TOMBO: I'm plannin' on flyin' this thing during most of my summer vacation. VWEE WOOO.

Wind blows and Kiki's skirt flutters. He pedals forcefully but the propeller doesn't move very fast. Kiki chuckles.

KIKI: …ha ha.

Tombo gets off his bike. He approaches Kiki. The propeller slows down.

TOMBO: Miss Witch, I got a great idea. Why don't we go down to the beach where that dirigible landed yesterday?

Kiki doesn't understand.

KIKI: Dirigible?

Tombo leans toward her.

TOMBO: Don't tell me you didn't hear about it?

KIKI:　　　I was sick.

Tombo grins.

TOMBO: Then we gotta see it! Let's do it!

Tombo's House/Gate Entrance

Tombo installs a rack onto his bicycle. Kiki holds the bike up.

KIKI:　　　We're going on this?
TOMBO: Why not? I have to practice all the time anyway. Gotta build up my legs.

He stands up, sticks his wrench into his pocket and straddles the saddle.

TOMBO: 'Kay. Ready?

Kiki looks at the rack and hesitates.

KIKI:　　　Um, mm-hmm (restrained voice).

She still darts over to the makeshift rack seat. She lifts her legs and the bike sways for a moment. She straddles onto it, shifts a little and settles onto it.

KIKI:　　　This is my first time on a bike.

Tombo looks back. Kiki is apprehensive.

TOMBO: Oh, boy. Just hold on. Brace the bike with your foot until I get her revved up. Let's go!

Tombo is carefree. He bends over and begins pedaling fiercely.

TOMBO: Kick off...now! Good!

The gears begin to spin, the chain flows. Tombo's feet move faster and faster.
Tombo pedals away. The wind only affects Kiki's skirt and hair though.
Tombo pedals away fiercely.

TOMBO: Ooh!

In spite of her uncomfortable position, Kiki presses the bike with her fingertips.
The bike begins to sway forward.
Tombo looks intense as he pedals away. The bike trudges along, slower than someone walking.

KIKI:　　　Should I get off?
TOMBO: No!

Tombo struggles. The bike plods along pathetically.

Hill

A man walking up a steep hill. He stares at the propeller plane at the center right. The propeller plane wavers forward. The man bursts out laughing.

MAN:　　　Ha ha.　Ha ha ha ha, ha ha ha.

Once Tombo's bike catches the slope though, it speeds up O.O.F.
Tombo's bike-plane whizzes down the slope.

Tombo pedaling away. Tombo's bike-plane enters the frame from the front left where the hill street joins the car road.
Tombo's bike dashes out onto the road. They enter from right corner and shoot off. The road rushes by. The blue sea horizon expands. They are whizzing by!!

Their P.O.V. There's a cliff below the road. Waves. The seaside car road. Tombo's bike-plane races through.
A car approaches and honks.

(S.E.) BEEP BEEP

Tombo's absolutely devoted to the task.
Kiki turns around. The car enters frame. A woman is driving.
The children in the backseat are watching them. They cheer on as they skim by. They are shouting and waving.　Kiki waves back at them.

KIDS:　　　Hey, look at that! Whoa!

Kiki looks cheerful. Her cheeks are red.
Tombo pedals away and shouts.

TOMBO: Lean your body to the inside when we go around the curve!
KIKI:　　　Why?!

Kiki doesn't understand. Tombo quickly explains.

TOMBO: Because, otherwise, we're gonna have trouble turning.

They're approaching the curve.
Tombo shouts at the right moment.

TOMBO: Now!

Kiki then leans over to the far right.
Tombo's bike-plane then tips far. It enters the curve, making a sharp-banked turn. Kiki's counterweight barely prevents them from dashing off the cliff.

TOMBO: Great! You're doin' fine.

Tombo shouts. She's getting used to this. Kiki sits up, then waits, preparing to lean to the far right. Tombo continues pedaling away.

They roar toward the next curve.

(S.E.) WHOOSH

They speed down the road. The seaside at their side.

(S.E.) FSSSHHH

Kiki leans over inside (This beats flying on a broom!!).　They race down the street.

Tombo's bike plane approaches the curve.

TOMBO: Now put your weight into it again. That's it! We're quite a team!

Their course is straight now. Kiki gets up.

They race by another building on the beach.

KIKI:　　　…!!

Kiki discovers something in the distance and leans over.

The dirigible makes an emergency landing. There are boats and cars in the area. More trees. Kiki sounds excited, too.

KIKI:　　　That's the dirigible, right?
TOMBO: Right!

The two suddenly stunned.

BOTH:　　　!!!

A black car comes at them. A sharp honk.

(S.E.) BEEP BEEP

It comes rushing at them, filling up the frame.

TOMBO: Whoa! Whoa!

The car charges forward from the center middle. Collision course!! Then suddenly the bike floats upward and skims over the car.
The car sways, then speeds by.

Tombo's bike plane still floats in the air. It manages to stay up in the air. It continues flying. Tombo cries out.

TOMBO: We're flying!

Kiki is surprised, too.
A castle-walled building on the beach park street. The traffic seems busier.

(S.E.) BEEP BEEP

A large truck approaches.
A sports car emerges from behind the truck!!

(S.E.) VRRROOM.

The two are once again stunned.

TOMBO: Oh, my gosh!

Tombo's bike plane rushes in from the right.

(S.E.) VROOM

Tombo's bike plane floats and climbs over the fence.
The large truck roars by. Tombo's bike plane descends to the front left O.O.F. Other cars pass by. The two fly up. The beach park spreads out. They float in the sky. Tombo keeps on pedaling.

(S.E.) KRAK

The propeller flies off, spinning away O.O.F. Tombo looks at it.

TOMBO: Oh, boy!

The propeller spins off, flying away like a butterfly.

Beach Park

People sunbathing on the lawn are bewildered.

PEOPLE: Hey! Watch it!

Tombo's bike plane crash-lands, bouncing off to the bottom left O.O.F.

(S.E.) KLAK KLAK KLAK KLAK

The bike descends the lawn. Its wheels are bent out of shape as it sways.
It rattles forward and comes out onto a flat area where it makes a sharp turn, throwing off Kiki and Tombo.
Kiki rolls on the grass and stops. She quickly looks up.

Kiki is flat on his back. The bike is bent out of shape, its front wheel still spinning. In the distance, lovers are taking walks.
Tombo manages to raise his head.

TOMBO: Ow…

Kiki gets up and rushes over to Tombo who's trying to get up.

KIKI: What happened, Tombo? Are you okay?
TOMBO: Yeah. Are you?
KIKI: I'm okay.

She's not so concerned now and suddenly bursts out laughing instead.

KIKI: …hee…

She's trying to restrain herself, but she can't.

KIKI: Hee hee…ha ha ha ha.
Hee hee ha ha ha.

She looks up and chuckles. It's her first unrestrained laughter.
She looks up and laughs hard.
Tombo is bewildered.

KIKI: (O.O.F.) Hee hee hee.
Ha ha ha.

Tombo stands up. Kiki can't stop laughing. Tombo is still bewildered.

KIKI: (O.O.F.) Ha ha ha.

The laughter's contagious. Tombo smiles.

TOMBO: Do I really look that funny?

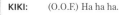

KIKI: I'm sorry, but when we flew up…

Kiki rubs her eyes while laughing. She turns toward him and tries to speak but her voice is still trembling.

KIKI: …I was so scared. Ha ha ha.

She laughs again. Tombo bursts out laughing too.

TOMBO: Ha ha ha…Yeah, me too.

Tombo asks her.

TOMBO: Was it your magic that made us stay up?

Kiki turns around.

KIKI: I'm not sure. Anything's possible.

Then she looks at the bike behind them.

KIKI: Your bike's a real mess.

Tombo turns around, but sees something in the air. The propeller gently descends from the blue sky. Kiki watches it. too.

TOMBO: My propeller! I have to go get it, Kiki. Will you keep an eye on my bike for me?

Tombo says and runs off, but then he stumbles O.O.F. Kiki is concerned.

KIKI: What went wrong?

Tombo limps along.

TOMBO: I think I pedaled too hard.

KIKI: …

Kiki's hair blows in the wind. She smiles as she watches Tombo. She walks to the right O.O.F.

Beach Park/Beach

(S.E.) FSSHH FSSHH

Waves against the shore. The serene sea. A large passenger ship passes by.

The dirigible makes an emergency landing onto the beach. Numerous cords secure it to the grass beyond the sand. Cars and boats in the area. Shadows in motion.

Tombo and Kiki sit on the grass below observing the giant silver airship. The bike and propeller sit next to them. They are resting.

TOMBO: How great would it be to go around the world in a dirigible like that.

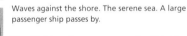

Buildings behind them on the beachfront road. Ancient castle wall and the clock tower further in the distance.
Tombo look at Kiki and asks.

TOMBO: Of course, you were flying since you were very young, huh?

KIKI: Well, yes, since I was a baby. My mother used to take me with her. She taught me never to be scared.

Kiki speaks in earnest. Tombo listens attentively.

TOMBO: Gosh. You're so lucky, Kiki. I wish I could fly.

Tombo envies her. He looks at her.

TOMBO: People like you can just fly away on a broomstick. But me? Vrrr vrrr (imitates propeller whirring)!!

That's all I can do.

KIKI: Ha ha...

Kiki smiles. She becomes pensive as she looks ahead and gazes at the sea. At the risk of sounding pretentious, she explains.

KIKI: Flying used to be fun until I started doing it for a living.

TOMBO: Hey, wait. You can't not enjoy flying. You're a witch!

His attitude is innocuous, she's not offended. Kiki smiles at him.

KIKI: I know. I still feel that way though.

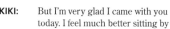

She looks ahead, then shrugs.

KIKI: But I'm very glad I came with you today. I feel much better sitting by the beach.

They're having their first intimate conversation.

TOMBO: Why don't I bring you here whenever you want and train myself at the same time?

KIKI: You're a very nice person.

TOMBO: Huh? You just found that out?

KIKI: Sorry, but at first I thought you were such a clown.

TOMBO: You know, my mom says the same thing. "Don't be such a clown. Quit looking up at the sky and get back to your books."

KIKI: Ha ha ha.
BOTH: Ha ha ha ha.

They both laugh. They understand each other. Park road. A junk car comes at them, braking to a halt.

(S.E.) KREECH VROM!!

Girl D sitting on the hood. Everyone looks to the left.
Kiki and Tombo look like a couple. They look intimate.
Girl C calls.

GIRL C: (O.O.F.) Tombo.

(S.E.) VROMVROM

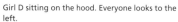

They turn around.
The car backs up toward them.
Girl D waves at them.

GIRL D: Guess what's up, Tombo!

Tombo looks back at her.

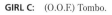

TOMBO: What?
GIRL C: (O.O.F.) Something really great! You're gonna love it! Come on over!

TOMBO: I'll be back in a sec, okay?

Tombo runs off the sand and onto the lawn O.O.F.
Kiki stands up.

KIKI: ...

She suddenly realizes something. She looks discouraged.
The girl sitting in the passenger's seat in the same car as girls C and D is the potpie girl.
Tombo runs up to them.

GIRL D: We're all gonna get to go for a ride in the blimp.

TOMBO: Really? Wow! That's great!
GIRL C: Hey, who's your friend?
TOMBO: (turns around) That's Kiki. I'll get her to come over.

Everyone looks at Kiki. The potpie girl gets up for a moment.

TOMBO: Hey, come over and meet the gang, Kiki.

Kiki looks stiff.

TOMBO: We're all goin' for a tour inside the Spirit of Freedom.
KIKI: Thanks, but I don't want to.

Tombo thinks she's only being shy so he runs up to her.

TOMBO: Oh, why not? It'll be fun.

The girls look her over calmly as if sizing her up. They're not being malicious though.

POTPIE GIRL: She made a delivery to my house on my birthday.
GIRL C: You mean, she's working at her age?
GIRL D: Well, I'll be.

Kiki looks as antagonistic as she did before. She doesn't look at Tombo. Tombo approaches her.

TOMBO: Come on. I'll introduce you to everybody.
KIKI: No thanks. See ya later.

Kiki gives him the cold shoulder. Kiki walks to the front left, up the grass O.O.F. Tombo gapes at her.

TOMBO: What's the matter?

Kiki marches on. Tombo, bewildered, watches her. He runs after her. Kiki walks on. Tombo catches up with her.

TOMBO: Hey! What are you so mad about?

Kiki won't even glance at him.

KIKI: I'm not mad at all, Tombo. I have a lot on my mind. So, please, just leave me alone.

TOMBO: ...!!

Tombo stops.
Kiki walks on O.O.F. Left behind, Tombo remains dumbstruck.

(S.E.) BEEP BEEP

Car honks.

GIRL D: Forget her, Tombo! Come on!

Kiki marches on. Tombo watches in a daze, bewildered.

Cliff Road

Vrroom. A car crosses the frame. Kiki walks on the cliff side of the road. Cars whiz by her.

(S.E.) VRRROOM

Kiki walks on the edge of the road. She walks down onto some rubble where the shoulder breaks off.

VRROOM. A large trailer skims past her. She falters, but then dodges the cars and returns to the road O.O.F.
Kiki hikes on.
It's a long way back home. There's no more traffic. It's quiet.

Bakery

Bakery at noon. It's quiet.

Attic Room

Kiki's room. It looks empty.

The door is shut. The door opens with a click. Kiki enters it without a word. She nudges the door shut from behind. She's lifeless.
Kiki shuffles into frame. She stops by the table, picks up the water pot, fills up her cup and drinks from it.

She puts down the cup and automatically turns on the radio. Noisy, superficial music.

(S.E.) Music

She shuts off the radio.
Kiki behind the window. She looks over at the window after turning off the radio. Kiki looks dejected.
She looks back, puts her hand down from the radio, and sighs deeply. She misses home.

KIKI: Whew.

Kiki walks up to the bed and keels over it. The bed rattles, then rests to a halt.
Kiki remains frozen. The room is quiet.

-Pause-

Jiji appears at the window and jumps onto the floor. He's very agile, the way a cat should be.

Floor below. Jiji slinks up to her, stops, and looks up, tilting his head.

JIJI: Meow–

Kiki lying on her bed. Jiji climbs up next to her. Jiji meows like a cat.

JIJI: Meow–

Kiki opens her eyes. She doesn't bother looking over at Jiji.

KIKI: Jiji, I think something's wrong with me. I meet a lot of people, and at first everything seems to be going okay.

KIKI: But then I start feeling like such an outsider. You should have seen how Tombo's friends looked at me.

Jiji's eyes are wide open. He's being strangely distant.
Like a cat, he acts indifferent and leaps onto the floor once Kiki's done talking.

KIKI: …?!

Kiki is bewildered. She raises her head and looks up.
Jiji runs under the window, leaps onto the sill and goes O.O.F.
Kiki is puzzled. This has never happened before. A brief pause.

KIKI: Oh. Some friend you are.

She mumbles and lies down.

Courtyard

On the wall in the afternoon. Lily gets Jiji's attention.

LILY: Meow–

Jiji comes. Lily leaps off the wall and disappears.
Jiji runs after her O.O.F.

Bakery

Kiki is tending the store alone.
Pedestrians are reflected in the display window.

Attic Room

Room in the evening. Kiki chews her food indifferently. Jiji shows up at the window. He skips onto the floor and approaches the table.

Kiki notices him.
Jiji slinks up to the table and starts licking the syrup on the pancake.
Kiki reacts, scolding him.

KIKI: Hey! You know, you can't be late for every meal just because you have a new girlfriend. And you can wash your plate yourself!

JIJI: Meow–

Jiji glances up.
Kiki is angry. Plates and silverware rattle on the table.

KIKI: Meow! Why are you talking like a cat?

JIJI: Meow–

Jiji looks down, then licks away the butter.
Kiki realizes something is wrong. She looks at him and addresses him slowly.

KIKI: (pause)…Jiji.

She's dumbfounded. Kiki leans forward.

KIKI: Oh, no! Talk to me, Jiji!

Jiji licks without responding. Kiki leans in more.

KIKI: You mean you can't speak anymore?

Jiji looks up with a sausage in his mouth. He turns around and skips onto the floor O.O.F.

KIKI: Jiji?

Jiji jumps onto the windowsill and exits.
Kiki is befuddled.

KIKI: What's going on with him? I can't understand anything he's trying to say.

She suddenly realizes.

KIKI: What if it means…Oh, my goodness!

She goes to her bed. The plates rattle, the chair topples. Crashing sound.

(S.E.) KRRSH KRRSH CHUDD!!

She runs up to the bed, grabs her broom and runs diagonally to the right O.O.F.

(S.E.) THUMP THUMP

She runs to the middle of the room. She clumsily straddles her broom. She concentrates then kicks against the floor. She floats as if she's about to fly. But then she falls.

(S.E.) KRRSH

She crashes onto the floor.
Kiki gets up again. Her eyes can't focus. She prepares again, shifting the broom. She concentrates. She waits. This time she doesn't kick her feet off the floor. Her clothes and hair flutter as she rises.

She drifts as if wading through water. She moves forward slowly and then sinks. She descends and falls to the floor.
Kiki slumps over. She's despondent.

KIKI: …

She doesn't know what to do.

193

Her trembling hands release the broom. CLOSE.

KIKI: I'm losing my witch's powers.

Vacant Lot/Night

Field at night. Kiki runs, straddling her broom. She's in the vacant lot behind the house. Kiki is practicing off the hill. She makes a running start, floats up, barely skims above the ground, then loses her buoyancy and ends up running downward O.O.F.

Kiki climbs up the field. A car passes on the road above.

KIKI: HUFF HUFF HUFF…

She's panting. She looks back, straddles the broom and runs.

She runs down the hill. Because she's straddling the broom, she's slightly bow-legged.
She kicks off the ground and floats slightly. She floats several meters upward but then lands. She continues running downward. She leaps up again, but then lands. She runs and skips up.

Kiki skims above the surface at the bottom of the field.

After landing, she runs bow-legged, then suddenly flips over and disappears into a recess.

KIKI: Aah! Whoa! Ooh!

Kiki's stupefied. She sits up and picks up the broom.

KIKI: Oh!

Her broom is broken in two. Kiki is speechless.

Kiki climbs out of the recess. She walks with her broken broom O.O.F.

Clothesline/Next Morning

Osono looks out from behind the clothesline in the morning light.

OSONO: What do you mean?

Kiki has told Osono about her dilemma. She hasn't slept at all. She has an odd, transparent look on her face.

OSONO: You haven't lost your magic, have you?
KIKI: It's become very weak, so I… (she glances down) Well, I think I've got to take a break from my delivery work. But I promise I'll be really good with my work in the bakery…

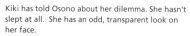

She stops. Then looks up seriously.

KIKI: …so please let me stay in the room upstairs!

Osono realizes how serious Kiki's situation is. She inquires.

OSONO: Well, that's no problem. I'll bet your powers come back after you've had some rest.

No one wants to know this more than Kiki does. She glances away.

KIKI: I really don't know. Maybe if I make a new broom.

The kitchen door opens and the husband leaps out. He runs to the front left O.O.F. He runs for the yard fence. He grabs the fence and calls for Osono.

HUSBAND: Hey! Look at that!

He points at the sky. Kiki and Osono look up.

A giant dirigible slowly glides by in the morning light. The husband waves his hat.
The dirigible floats past Kiki.
Kiki looks on, conscious of how she can't fly anymore.

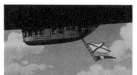

Someone waving from the gondola. It might be Tombo.

Rooftop

Jiji and Lily on the rooftop. The dirigible disappears behind them.

(S.E.) WOM WOM WOM

Clothesline

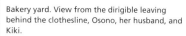

Bakery yard. View from the dirigible leaving behind the clothesline, Osono, her husband, and Kiki.

Tombo sits by the bay window, making a phone call. It's getting dark outside.
Kiki answers his call.

TOMBO: Hi, Kiki? It's me, Tombo. Did you see me today? I was wavin' at ya from the dirigible, 'cause the captain let me come into the control cabin during the test run. Boy, did I have a cool time!

Bakery Interior

Kiki answers the store phone. She mumbles back.

TOMBO: (O.O.F.) Hello? Kiki? Are you there?

KIKI: Please don't call me anymore.
TOMBO: (O.O.F.) What did ya say? I can barely hear ya. You know what the captain said? He'd like to meet ya…

Uninterested, Kiki hangs up on him.

(S.E.) KLIK

Tombo's House

Tombo is bewildered. He shouts into the phone.

TOMBO: …?! What? Kiki?

Inside Bakery

Kiki wanders out of the bakery. Osono follows her into the hall O.O.F. Her husband crouches down to retrieve some bread.

OSONO: What's the matter, dear? Is there anything I can do for you?

Kiki has her hand on the door. She turns around and declares in a lucid tone.

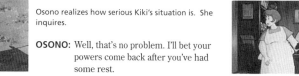

KIKI: I'm still in training to become a witch. If I lose my magic, that means I've lost absolutely everything.

She opens the door and slips out. The door clicks shut.

Attic Room

In the dark empty room, Kiki is carving away at a yew stick under the lamp. She rubs her eyes. She may be weeping. She continues carving.

Street/Noon

FADE IN

Someone walking a side street, the bright main street behind her. She's a young woman wearing shorts and a straw hat, carrying a large backpack. As she walks on, she looks down at a note in her hand, checking the building numbers on both sides of the street. It's the painter, Ursula.

Ursula asks for directions in front of the grocer. The owner comes out, examines the note, and points to his right as if saying, turn right there.

Bakery/Courtyard

Ursula enters the street, looks in, and then proceeds to the left.
Kiki exits, holding a bagful of bread, returning to her room. Ursula shouts.

URSULA: Kiki!

Kiki stops, bewildered. At first she doesn't realize who it is.

KIKI: …?

Ursula passes the three-wheeled truck, turns, and then approaches Kiki.

URSULA: Hey!
KIKI: Hi!

Kiki realizes it's Ursula as she approaches. Kiki also steps towards her.

URSULA: Well, since you didn't come and visit me, I thought I'd come here and visit you.

KIKI: I'm sorry.
URSULA: Well, that's sort of a white lie. I need to do some shopping too.

Kiki is happy to see her.

KIKI: Come on in, 'cause I'm done now, and I can take a break, okay?
URSULA: You better believe I will.
KIKI: Ha ha…

Ursula leans in, teasing her. Kiki is really glad to see her.

Attic Room

Ursula puts down her huge backpack onto the floor.

(S.E.) WHUDD

She gets up and puts her hand on the backpack. Kiki fills the basket on the table with the bagful of bread.

Ursula looks around.

URSULA: Nice place you have.
KIKI: Help yourself to some of these, and I'll go make us some tea.

Kiki offers the basket of bread. She takes the pot to the back. Ursula takes a piece of bread.

URSULA: No tea, thanks, but some milk if you have any.
KIKI: Sure.

Kiki replies O.O.F.

Ursula takes a bite and looks toward the window. She leans out as she continues chewing. She notices Jiji walking up to her.

URSULA: Hey there. Unbelievable. You're the spitting image of that stuffed cat. I bet your name's Jiji, right?

Jiji approaches her, hesitates, and then leaps past Ursula into the room.
Ursula watches Jiji enter as she turns around, leaning back on the sill. Simultaneously, Kiki enters frame and pours milk.

URSULA: So how's the delivery biz? You makin' any money?

Kiki stops.

KIKI: …

She puts down the cup of milk without a word. Ursula realizes something's wrong. Her eyes open wide.

URSULA: That bad, huh?
KIKI: I'm not working much now.
URSULA: (O.O.F.) Mm-hmm.

Kiki pours milk into Jiji's bowl, too. She puts the bottle on the table and crouches.
She offers the bowl to Jiji. She pushes it forward. Jiji begins lapping it up. He's just a normal cat now.

Ursula watches Jiji chew on the last piece of bread.

Attic Room/Late Night

They are sitting on the bed. Kiki is done explaining her situation.

URSULA: Hmm. I kind of thought you looked unhappy. I didn't know things like that happened to witches.

Kiki doesn't respond.
Ursula sits up and walks up to the broomstick. She grabs it and turns around.

URSULA: Hey! Why don't you come and stay at my cabin?
KIKI: Huh?

Kiki raises her face. She doesn't understand Ursula's train of thought. Ursula insists.

URSULA: It'll probably make you feel better. Your boss would let you have a break. (looks at Jiji) How about it, kitty cat? Wanna come? Hmm?
JIJI: …

Jiji sits on the pillow. He drowsily opens his eyes, but then closes them.
Ursula leans back.

URSULA: Rather be with your girlfriend, huh? (To Kiki) Come on, girl. Why not? We'll leave now.

Kiki isn't up for it. Her eyes wide open as she nods ambivalently.

Rooftop/Noon

Jiji climbing up to Lily on the rooftop.

Street/Noon

Kiki and Ursula pass the café filled with young men and women. The tree shade is dark. Ursula marches on cheerfully, chatting away. Kiki laughs.

Bus Terminal

Bus terminal. A small bus parked in the corner. Ursula runs in from the front left.

URSULA: The bus is leaving!!

She turns and calls on Kiki behind her. Kiki enters frame. As they run another bus runs behind them from the left.

(S.E.) VRRROOM

Inside Bus

Back of the bus. Ursula goes to the back and plops down. Kiki enters frame too and sits near her. Ursula shakes her backpack loose.

(Kiki smiling. She's not as preoccupied as she was in her room.)
The conductor closes the door. The driver puts the bus into gear and the bus moves forward.

(S.E.) RRRR RRRR

Ursula leans against her backpack. She blows a bubble with her gum, offering Kiki a piece. Kiki smiles and takes it. Ursula spills them all over the place.

KIKI: Ahh!

They cross a bridge.

Bus Stop

(S.E.) VRRROOOM

The bus leaves the stop.
They climb the grass hill.
Ursula struggles with her heavy backpack. Kiki enters the frame. She's pushing on the backpack. Ursula turns back, smiling.

Kiki keeps on pushing.

Hilltop

Hilltop overlooking forest and ranches. Ursula and Kiki climb up to it. They're racing.

BOTH: (O.O.F.) Ha ha ha ha ha…

Kiki is behind.

URSULA: Okay, now I'm officially exhausted.

She stops, panting. Kiki climbs up and turns around to view everything below.

KIKI: It's beautiful here.

She's amazed. The wind blows against her face. She can see the shining sea. She looks up. The natural surroundings help her get over her sullen feelings. She turns around and skips toward Ursula O.O.F.

Street

Kiki runs toward Ursula who's hitchhiking on the side of the road.

Ursula extends her right arm and sticks her thumb out. Kiki looks to her right. Approaching car.

(S.E.) VRRROOM

Passenger car passes by them.
They're surprised.

(S.E.) RRRRR

They look over. Ursula looks at her.

URSULA: (turning around) Must have been blinded by two beautiful girls in front of him.

KIKI: Ha ha…

Ursula mutters (the passenger vehicle vanishes). She looks at the road. Still smiling, Kiki looks too. Another car appears.

Kiki raises her hand. Kiki also imitates Ursula and raises her hand.
Approaching car.

(S.E.) VRRROOM
(S.E.) RRR RRR RRR

An old truck passes by, fumes trailing behind. Kiki gapes at it. Ursula covers her face.
The truck climbs the hill then screeches to a halt. It won't stop fuming.

(S.E.) KREECH PUFF

Ursula excited.

URSULA: …!!

She looks at Kiki and runs to the front right. Kiki also follows O.O.F.

Forest Road

Truck passes forest.

(S.E.) RRR RRR RRR

Kiki and Ursula sit in the passenger seat.

Truck

The front seat. Ursula's been listening to the old man.

URSULA: You really thought I was a boy?

The old man smiles.

OLD MAN: Well, it's the way you're dressed and all.

Ursula lifts her knees and groans.

URSULA: Tell me. What kind of a boy has these legs, mister?
KIKI: Ha ha…

Kiki laughs. Superimposition on glass.

Forest

They wave. The old man responds and drives through the forest O.O.F.
The start walking up the forest trail. It was a fun ride. Kiki is feeling cheerful now.

Log Cabin/Entrance

Ursula's cabin. Several crows perched on the roof. Some fly down. From the right and left Ursula and Kiki walk up.

KIKI: You get along with the crows.
URSULA: Yep, we've become real close friends.

KIKI: Wow!

URSULA: Hello, everybody. I'm home again.

She walks up to the cabin as the crows welcome her. Kiki also stops and says hi.

KIKI: Good afternoon. Um, I wanna say I'm sorry.

Ursula walks O.O.F. A crow caws.

CROW: KAHH–

Ursula puts down her backpack at the door, grabs the bucket by the door, and comes out onto the terrace.

URSULA: Why don't you go inside, and I'll go get some water?

She hands her key to Kiki as she enters the frame and then walks to the left O.O.F. Kiki steps onto the terrace and watches as she approaches the door.

Log Cabin/Room

Cabin Interior. Kiki opens the lock with the key.

(S.E.) CLATCH

Kiki opens the door. Then she hoists Ursula's backpack into the room. She sees something in front of her.

KIKI: …!!

Transfixed, she puts down the backpack. As usual, the room is messy, but there's a large painting on an easel in the middle of the room. (TRACK UP) It's an imaginary world full of life.

Kiki walks up to the canvas. She gazes at the large painting.
Various parts of the painting. Cow flying through the heavens. The crows and forest. Pegasus and a girl. She examines the entire image.

She's mesmerized. Ursula passes outside by the window, holding a bucket as she descends. She sees Kiki staring at the painting and addresses her as she moves to the left O.O.F.

URSULA: Like it?

Kiki looks at Ursula outside the frame.

KIKI: Yes.

Ursula hoists the bucket onto the stove.

URSULA: I have to say I became inspired after the first time we met.

To the front left, she approaches Kiki, but she's staring at the canvas. Kiki doesn't understand. Her eyes open wide.

KIKI: …?

She enters frame by her and looks up.

URSULA: But…I really haven't got the face right.

Kiki looks at the painting at the end of the shot. Ursula looks at Kiki.

URSULA: I've been waiting for you to come back so I can try again.

Kiki finally realizes the girl's based on her.

KIKI: You mean that's me?

URSULA: Sure is.

Ursula crouches down and picks up her sketchbook from the floor. She points at the chair outside the frame.

URSULA: You know, you'd make my life a lot easier if you'd model for me.

Kiki is flustered. Ursula insists.

KIKI: But I'm not very beautiful. What do you want me to do that for?

Ursula looks amused. She bursts out laughing.

URSULA: …!! HA HA HA HA…

Kiki is bewildered. Ursula leans over.

URSULA: Come on, Kiki. You have got a great face. You're very pretty.

Ursula takes Kiki to the left O.O.F. as if embracing her with her sketchbook.

Sketching

The sketch. Ursula's hand drawing a girl who vaguely resembles Kiki. She traces the eyes and then adds the diagonal lines for her cheeks.

Ursula draws fast. Kiki sits still.

URSULA: Raise your chin up a little. Look straight ahead. Now, don't move.

These directions make Kiki hesitate. Ursula keeps on drawing with concentration. She looks and draws, draws and looks. While drawing, she speaks.

URSULA: Painting and magical powers seem very much the same. Sometimes I'm unable to paint a thing.

Kiki turns around.

KIKI: You mean it? Then what? What happens?

URSULA: (O.O.F.) Kiki, please don't move. It's hard to draw a moving target.

KIKI: …

Kiki's eyes open wide. She sits still though. After pausing, she speaks. She's somber without being uncomfortable.

KIKI: Without even thinking about it, I used to be able to fly. Now I'm trying to look inside myself to find out how I did it. But I just can't figure it out.

URSULA: …

Ursula stops drawing and looks up at Kiki. (She catches a glimpse of Kiki's pensive expression and realizes that's what she wanted.) She closes her sketchbook, opens it for another sheet and starts drawing large strokes.

URSULA: You know, could be you're working at it too hard. Maybe you should just take a break.

Kiki shares her innermost feelings.

She glances over at Ursula and looks straight ahead.
She droops her head.

KIKI: Yeah, but still, if I can't fly.

URSULA: (O.O.F.) Then stop trying. Take long walks. Look at the scenery. Doze off at noon. Don't even think about flying.

KIKI: …

Kiki forgets she's modeling and looks over at Ursula. Ursula continues sketching away.

URSULA: And then, pretty soon, you'll be flying again.

Kiki faces Ursula.

KIKI: You think my problems will…

URSULA: Go away? That's right.

She rests her hand, looks up and confidently reassures her.

URSULA: It's gonna be fine. I promise.

Kiki looks back at Ursula.

KIKI: …

She assumes her pose. How nice it would be to fly again, she thinks to herself…

The setting sun shines on the birch trees. The lake and sky. They take a walk. Ursula is showing Kiki something.

Cabin Interior

Night. Cabin interior. Ursula flipping an omelette on her frying pan. Kiki smiling for a change. Ursula and Kiki are getting ready for bed as they continue chatting. Lamp and nightcap brandy on the floor.

URSULA: When I was your age, I'd already decided to become an artist. I loved to paint so much. I'd paint all day until I fell asleep right at my easel.

She looks up.

URSULA: And then one day, for some reason, I just couldn't paint anymore.

Kiki listens attentively.

URSULA: (O.O.F.) I tried and tried, but nothing I did seemed any good.
KIKI: Huh.

Ursula rests her chin on the pillow.

URSULA: They were copies of paintings I'd seen somewhere before and not very good copies either. I just felt like I'd lost my ability.

She lifts her cup but doesn't drink. She looks serious.

KIKI: That sounds like me.

Kiki seems to have an understanding of Ursula now.
Ursula sips on her nightcap and then smiles.

URSULA: It's exactly the same…but then I found the answer.

Kiki listens up.

URSULA: (O.O.F.) You see, I hadn't figured out what or why I wanted to paint. I had to discover my own style.
KIKI: Mm-hmm.

Kiki nods without a word.
The lamp glows in this intimate setting. Ursula rests her chin on her hands and says as if to change the subject.

URSULA: When you fly, you rely on what's inside of you, don't you?
KIKI: Uh-huh. We fly with our spirit.

Ursula raises her shoulders a little.

URSULA: Trusting your spirit! Yes, yes! That's exactly what I'm talkin' about.

Lamp on the floor. Drawn to its flame, a small moth bumps into the glass.

URSULA: (O.O.F.) That same spirit is what makes me paint and makes your friend bake.

Ursula looks off into the distance.

URSULA: But we each need to find our own inspiration, Kiki. Sometimes it's not easy.

Kiki is pensive, but looks reinvigorated.

KIKI: I guess I never gave much thought to why I wanted to do this. I got so caught up in all the training and stuff. Maybe I have to find my own inspiration.

Ursula looks up.

KIKI: (O.O.F.) But am I ever gonna find it? And is it worth all the trouble?

Ursula smiles.

URSULA: Well, for example, there were quite a few times…when I thought of painting something over that painting.

KIKI: But it ended up being so great.

The Pegasus and the girl seen from below. Ursula looks back at her cheerfully.

URSULA: So I guess it's worth it. Today when I saw you I thought, I wanna paint! You've got such a great face.

Kiki taken aback. She pulls back.

KIKI: That's why I came?
URSULA: Hey, well, it's better than you cleaning my floor again.

Ursula chuckles.
Kiki shrugs and laughs.

KIKI: HA HA HA

URSULA: (O.O.F.) Let's turn out the lights and go to sleep.
KIKI: Okay.

Kiki leans over and puts her cup down on the floor. She climbs onto the bed.

KIKI: Sorry about taking your bed from you.
URSULA: Aw, no problem.

Ursula snuggles under the sleeping bag, stretches out, lifts the lamp cover and blows out the flame.

URSULA: Whew.

It's dark. Kiki fidgets under the sheets, then addresses Ursula below.

KIKI: So you really think I'll fly again?
URSULA: (O.O.F.) Sure. You'll just have to wait for the right inspiration to come along. You understand?

KIKI: Uh-huh.

She smiles, nods, and closes her eyes. FADE OUT.

TV Screen

Black and white television set in Osono's house. The dirigible flying in the air.

TV REPORTER: And there it is, folks, the *Spirit of Freedom...*

...recently downed in a spectacular forced landing due to torrential rains just outside the city limits. Well, it's been repaired. It is now in final preparation.

Husband with his morning paper and coffee. The store phone rings.

(S.E.) BRRING BRRING

Husband turns around because Osono won't answer the phone. Then she answers it.

OSONO: (O.O.F.) Yes? Good Cooking Pan Bakery.

Inside Bakery

Osono answers phone. The bakery is bright inside.

OSONO: Kiki! How are you? Well, you take plenty of time coming home. Oh, and by the way...

Roadside

Kiki calling from a phone booth. Ursula is trying to thumb a ride for Kiki.

OSONO: (O.O.F.) ...that older woman you made a delivery for? She has another delivery for you. I said I wasn't sure you could do it.

Car ignores Ursula. Ursula glares back at it.

Inside Bakery

Osono speaks cheerfully.

OSONO: She was really very insistent. What do you think, Kiki? Great! Stop there on your way back. Bye.

KIKI: Bye!

Receiver clicks.

(S.E). KLIK

(Osono believes Kiki has recovered.)

Roadside

Kiki hitches a ride. After a brief pause, it moves on.
Ursula waves goodbye at her.

Mansion/Long Shot

Quiet residential street. Kiki steps off the tram and onto the small platform. Its bell rings. The tram moves on.

(S.E.) DING DING

Kiki crosses the street.

Mansion/Entrance

Barsa opens the door where Kiki stands cheerfully. She curtsies politely.

KIKI: Afternoon, ma'am.
BARSA: Well, well, we've been expecting you.

Barsa invites her in. Kiki enters to the front left O.O.F. Barsa closes the door behind her.

Study

Watching the television installed on the study shelf, the lady turns, acknowledging Kiki's arrival with a smile as she spins (on the spinning chair).

Television news coverage (the coverage continues throughout the following shots).

TV REPORTER: There are less than five minutes to takeoff now. The local fire department and the Coast Guard stand ready.

The old lady looks at Kiki as she enters the frame from the left. She curtsies. The old lady welcomes her.

KIKI: Um, it's very nice to see you again, ma'am.
OLD LADY: I'm glad you came. Please excuse me for not standing. My legs are bothering me more than usual.

She leans over to the door and addresses her maid.

OLD LADY: Barsa, bring the package now.

The maid rushes in from the convalescent room, carrying a box of cake.

BARSA: Gosh, I hope it hasn't taken off.
OLD LADY: Not yet.

Maid enters frame from the back left and moves up to the far side of the table.
The old lady addresses Kiki.

OLD LADY: Barsa is absolutely mad about lighter-than-air travel.
BARSA: I'm the adventuresome type.

The maid puts the dessert box on the table and hurries back to the television.

OLD LADY: Could you turn it down, please? (She looks at Kiki.) Would you do me a favor and open the box?

The maid lowers the TV volume.
Lady's over-the-shoulder shot at Kiki.

KIKI: Yep.

She steps up and opens the box. The cake inside surprises her.

KIKI: …!!

CLOSE on cake. It's a chocolate cake, its white chocolate topping a silhouette of Kiki and her name. Her ribbon is strawberry jam.
She looks up at the lady.

KIKI: I don't get it.

The lady smiles and teases her.

OLD LADY: Would you please bring this to a young delivery girl? She was kind to me and a very big help.

KIKI: Kiki is speechless. She doesn't know what to say.

OLD LADY: It's my way of saying thank you. Ah, yes, and can you find out when her next birthday is? Then I can bake her another one. Will you handle this very special delivery, Kiki?

Still bewildered, Kiki slowly looks down at the cake. She's about to burst into tears. Silence. The lady smiles, looking at her. She understands why Kiki's so quiet. She speaks to her gently.

OLD LADY: Don't cry.

Kiki shifts the box lid to her left hand to wipe away her tears. Suddenly, she says cheerfully with a twinkle in her eye.

KIKI: Of course I will! And maybe the young girl will want to know the lady's birthday because she'll be able to give her a present to repay her!

OLD LADY: You've got a deal.

She exclaims and they laugh together.

BOTH: Ha ha.

Barsa is alarmed. She points out.

People being blown by the gust. Paper and hats fly off. People running around.
Barsa's hand enters and turns up the volume loud.

(S.E.) RRRR KRAK KRAK

Kiki fixes her eyes on the TV set. The lady turns around.

(FSSHHH) The sound is cut off.

The maid fiddles with the TV set. The reception is intermittent with static. Images of the lopsided dirigible. Intermittent voices.

PEOPLE: AHHH AIEEE

(S.E.) FSSSHHH

People running. PAN across the sky. It's all a blur. The maid is transfixed. The lady asks what's going on. Kiki closes the box.

OLD LADY: What happened?
BARSA: Oh, there's been a terrible accident.

The maid turns around and answers. The sound returns. The maid looks back. They're shocked by the sight.

The stern of the dirigible drifts with the wind. People running away. Paper everywhere. The gondola approaches the broadcast van.

(S.E.) Crashing noise

(S.E.) KRRSH KRR KRR

It crashes, then pulls away. An odd image appears and the image turns into static.

BARSA: Oh, darn this old thing! And just when it was getting good!

They stare at the TV. The tube projects strange images, then horizontal lines appear with intermittent sound.
The maid fiddles with the set.

Kiki is worried about Tombo.

OLD LADY: Midsummer is always when these winds come. They'll be hitting us any minute.

A gust comes in as she speaks.

(S.E.) RRRRR

Kiki and the lady look to the right.

The branches outside shake, and the windowsills rattle. The curtains flutter.

(S.E.) KLAK KLAK FWEEE

OLD LADY: It'll pass quickly. Don't worry.
BARSA: (O.O.F.) Oh, goody! It's back on. Look!

Barsa exclaims. Kiki and the lady look at the TV. The image is shaky. People seem to be making an attempt to secure the rope.

(S.E.) FSSSH

A clear image suddenly appears. The maid leans in.

BARSA: Oh, look at that. It's completely upside down.

The frame. People rushing around frantically. Suddenly the TV reporter's voice comes in. He's beat up, but holds onto his mic. The people rushing forward behind him.

TV REPORTER: Freak winds blowing in from the sea! It has broken loose from its mooring ropes.

Kiki steps up to the TV. The maid is excited.

BARSA: My, my. How terrible.

TV screen. The stern of the ship points upward. The rudder and part of the ship are destroyed.

TV REPORTER: A desperate last-ditch effort is being made to tie the dirigible to the ground and keep it from drifting into the air.

A ground shot. The rope base, police car, and people. Civilians and sailors rushing in. People are being dragged upward.

TV REPORTER: But it's extremely doubtful whether or not this can actually be done.

Kiki tries to locate Tombo.

She sees something. She leans in. The screen. The human weight begins to crumble.

TV REPORTER: Oh, no, no! It's useless! The tremendous lifting power of the helium balloon is lifting the police patrol car-

Someone at the top leaps off. Others follow, revealing Tombo. Kiki is horrified.

KIKI: That's Tombo! That's my friend hanging on that rope.
BARSA: Huh?

The dirigible rapidly rises. The men give up and let go. The rope ascends quickly. Tombo goes O.O.F.

TV REPORTER: It's being lifted as though it were a toy!

The rope drifts to the left, followed by the police car lifted up into the air.

Tombo hangs from the rope. The dirigible flies upward with the police car dangling. The TV reporter. The ascending dirigible, *Spirit of Freedom* is upside-down.

TV REPORTER: Oh, no, there's a young boy hanging onto the cable! He's being lifted away together with the police car! I don't believe what I'm seeing. The dirigible is being blown towards town! I'm told our remote crew has escaped injury…

KIKI: (frozen) Tombo!!

Barsa and the lady look at Kiki and then the TV set. The lady stares at the TV.

OLD LADY: Are you sure it's your friend, my dear?

Kiki turns to the lady.
KIKI: I have to go!

Barsa panics. She looks back and forth at Kiki leaving and the TV set.

Mansion Gate

Gate covered with flowers. Kiki runs down the stairs and out of the gate. She dashes to the right on the sidewalk. The leaves and flower petals are scattered all over the ground from the gust. Back shot of Kiki running by the boulevard trees of the elegant mansion district. She's fast.

Main Street

Rows of cars. People. Everyone looking at the sky. PAN UP. People on the city castle walls too.

The *Spirit of Freedom* drifts by. Tombo and the police car are dangling from it.

Dirigible

Giant shadow sweeps the streets. People are moving around the lawn and parking lot behind the castle walls. Tombo desperately hangs on. He's losing his grip.
The captain inside the gondola yells through his megaphone.

CAPTAIN: Hold on there, son! Just hold your grip steady!

He yells out instructions inside the gondola.

CAPTAIN: Release the helium from the tail! Quick!

Tombo can't last much longer.

TOMBO: URGH…URGH…Oh!

He slips and stops. He crashes into the police car.

(S.E.) KRRSH KRAK KRAK

The bumper is torn off from the impact and the patrol car falls O.O.F. Tombo holds on as the patrol car crashes into the bright blue pool of the hotel. The water sprays all over.

Backstreet

Shopping district hill. Everyone who's heard the news is outside watching the sky.
Kiki is running. She's pretty worn out as the children pass her. She runs O.O.F.

KIKI: HUFF HUFF HUFF.

She grunts as she runs.

(S.E.) EEYOO EEYOO EEYOO-

Suddenly, ambulance sirens. She looks up.

Hilltop

People agitated. Cars pulled over, people everywhere looking up at the sky. The lamp of the ambulance driving beyond them.
Kiki enters from the center. She climbs up the hill. People rush around.

(S.E.) EEYOO EEYOO

Main Street

Crowd gazing at the sky, others running around.

CROWD: Hmph! Gotta see this! What's going on?

Kiki almost crashes into someone, but she can't be bothered. She follows everyone else's gaze.
The silver ship drifts to the left up above beyond the street.

Everyone gazing up. Traffic jam. People running. Slight PAN UP to show the entire inverted dirigible. The roofs block any sight of Tombo.

KIKI: Tombo!!

Kiki sounds frantic. She hears a car radio and runs to the front right O.O.F.
(the car radio broadcast blended in with the crowd noise)

The driver leaves the car radio on. Kiki shouts at him as she enters from the back right.

KIKI: Sir, is there any word about the boy?

The driver turns to her.

DRIVER: All I know is that the radio said that the police car dropped into a pool.

Kiki runs O.O.F.

Everyone is out on the streets. Kiki weaves her way through them. People are shocked, some are enjoying the sight. Kiki bumps against a middle-aged woman, then a maid, and runs O.O.F. Kiki comes out onto a car street as she runs between the cars. She goes to the right back. The tail of the dirigible vanishes behind the rooftops.

Kiki enters frame from front right. Crowd. Kiki goes O.O.F. The dirigible tail also drifts O.O.F.

(S.E.) EEYOO EEYOO (the siren continues)

Kiki runs, skimming by everyone. People on the rooftops.

KIKI:　　　HUFF HUFF.

Kiki runs down the car street. The crowd is divided in two as if to make way for Kiki.

The fire truck siren comes from behind entering the frame, closing in on her. The fire truck megaphone warns everyone.

FIREMAN: (O.O.F.) Stay out of the street! Get on the sidewalks! You there! Young lady! Don't block the street! Clear the area! Do not block the street!

Kiki runs in from the right and stops by grabbing the column of a street lamp. The fire trucks rush past her.

(S.E.) EEYOO EEYOO EEYOO

Kiki looks up and pants. The sound of fire trucks rushing by her. An old man watches Kiki with concern.

OLD MAN: Are you all right, young lady?

Kiki looks at him and notices something at his feet.

KIKI:　　　…!!

The old man has a deck brush. (PAN UP) He appears to be a friendly janitor. Kiki goes up to him.

KIKI:　　　Please, sir, may I use your broom for a minute?

People behind her moving around to watch the dirigible.

OLD MAN: What?

The old man naturally hesitates. Kiki insists.

KIKI:　　　Please! I promise I'll bring it right back!

He's reluctant.

OLD MAN: Huh? I'm not gonna give you my broom.
KIKI:　　　Thank you very much!
OLD MAN: Hey!

She grabs the brush and comes out onto the street. She straddles it and assumes her flying position.

It's an embarrassing pose to take in front of a crowd.

KIKI:　　　…

Kiki concentrates intensely. She draws in her strength and constricts her body.

The old man is bewildered. Everyone stares at her. Kiki is in the middle of the street, straddling the brush in deep concentration. No wonder everyone's staring at her.

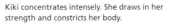

KIKI:　　　…

She can't hear a thing now. She doesn't care how she looks. Her only concern is flying.

Kiki pale. Her witch blood begins to flow and she looks intimidating.

The brush hairs start rustling and then shoot out rapidly as if sparked by electricity.

Everyone is amazed. The janitor is concerned, given how the brush is his tool.

Kiki's hair, ribbon and clothes also shoot out, then flutter. Kiki creates a gust that blows off the paper around her. Kiki slowly begins to rise. She's fluttering, but slowly begins to rise.

Kiki looks up. The fierce face of a witch. Her hair and clothes flutter.

She hisses.

KIKI:　　　Fly!!

A brief pause. Then she shoots upward O.O.F. Kiki flies up.
She curves off into a building wall, but she kicks off the building and flies to the left (O.O.F.).

The crowd gaze at her and cheer.

OLD MAN, CROWD:　Whoa!

Kiki flies at the roof window on the other side of the street. The surprised observers in the area watch her as she ricochets off a roof window and flies up into the sky.

The clock tower and dirigible can be seen beyond the rooftops.

City Sky

Kiki circles upward into the sky. She has her eyes on the dirigible as she fills up the frame.
Circling the sky, she flies toward the dirigible. She rapidly accelerates, then stops, and suddenly falls.

KIKI:　　　Oh!

Kiki begins falling.

Rooftop

Kiki continues falling. The boys watching the dirigible are alarmed.

(S.E.) KRRSH

She crashes and tumbles down the tin roof. She's strong enough to hold onto her brush though.

Kiki falls into the air toward the semi-circle courtyard. There's a crowded café below with parasol tables.

Café

Unaware of the emergency, people here are enjoying their drinks as Kiki falls.
(S.E.) VWOOSH
She weaves her way between the parasols and people, recovering her flight right before hitting ground, creating a gust to the front left.

PEOPLE: Did you see that?
Unbelievable! Flew up in the air!

Kiki shoots out into the passage outside the courtyard. She's soaring now. She zooms by bewildered pedestrians and comes out onto the street.

The Street

Kiki flies out above the traffic jam and crowd in the street. She rapidly ascends and soars up into the sky above the left building O.O.F.

In the Air

Kiki frantically tries to hold down the deck brush. She shouts at it. Speed up!!

KIKI: Come on, broom. Fly for me!!

Central Park

The central park. Cars are parked and people are running away. The giant dirigible shadow is sweeping toward them. The police cars are slow.

The giant dirigible drifts above the buildings facing the park.

TV Crew

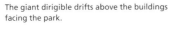

The roof of the building facing the park. A TV crew amongst the onlookers. The cars are parked while people move around.

TV REPORTER: (fast talking) Ladies and gentlemen, it appears that the blimp is heading directly for the clock tower! And, look, the young boy is safe, but he's clutching that rope for dear life! If the wind doesn't shift, the *Spirit of Freedom* will smash into the tower!

Dirigible

The *Spirit of Freedom* approaches the clock tower.

Tombo is visible.

The clock tower looms. Tombo on the bumper looks up and shouts. The keeper is in the tower.

TOMBO: We gotta get up higher or else we'll hit the tower, Captain!

The captain shouts through his megaphone from the overturned gondola.

CAPTAIN: There's not enough helium. Jump onto the tower before we hit!
TOMBO: Aye, aye, Captain!

Tombo responds. They approach the clock dial. Tombo looks ahead.

The keeper waves and shouts.

KEEPER: Hey there! Over here! Come on!

Tombo approaches him in the air.

TOMBO: Get outta the way! The blimp's gonna crash!
KEEPER: Grab a hold of this!

The keeper shouts, offering a brush.

Tombo enters the frame, approaching the clock dial. The bow crashes into the tower.

(S.E.) KRRSH KRRSH

It digs in. Tiles scatter.
Tombo tries to hold onto the dial as the frame shakes. People and cars below.

Tombo desperately clings to the dial, frantically searching for some support. The tiles come raining down from above. The dirigible bow continues digging into the top of the tower. The dome above sways. Fragments fall everywhere.

Tombo desperately clings to the building as the tiles comes raining down. He's hit.

(S.E.) KLAK

He lets go and frantically grabs the rope. He swings back O.O.F. He returns from the front, swinging into the frame. The bumper at his leg comes loose and falls.

City Sky

Kiki comes at him. There's a gust. Her eyes open wide.

The clock tower approaches. The buildings speed by on both sides.

The clock tower dome is nearly about to tip over.

Kiki frantically rushes in. She shouts at her broom.

KIKI: Hurry up!

She looks up and falls O.O.F. As she falls Kiki yells.

KIKI: Hey!

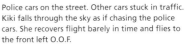

Police cars on the street. Other cars stuck in traffic. Kiki falls through the sky as if chasing the police cars. She recovers flight barely in time and flies to the front left O.O.F.

Kiki speeds past the police car like the wind. The policeman is speechless. Her behind is entirely exposed as she skims over the street, meandering a little. The clock tower approaches.

Clock Tower

The dirigible sticks up into the sky. Gas is leaking everywhere.

(S.E.) FSSH FSSH

PAN DOWN. It's squashed onto the tower. The dirigible and the rooftop TV crew in front.

Broadcast Location

Reporter on the rooftop. Onlookers.

TV REPORTER: We are listening to the sound of a helium gas leak! The condition of the boy is unknown, but from where I'm standing. Oh, no!

The reporter looks up and shouts.

TV REPORTER: It's falling!

While the camera slowly turns upward, people move. The dirigible breaks in the middle and the tail slowly falls. Gas is rapidly leaking.

(S.E.) KREEEK KRAK RRAK
FSSH KREEK KREEK

Reporter screams. He's surrounded by onlookers.

TV REPORTER: Too much gas has escaped. It's coming down!

Central Park

Rescue squad, police officers and onlookers panic and run.

CROWD: AHH! AIEEE

The shadow of the dirigible tail enters frame and sweeps over the entire area.

Roof of building facing the park. The shadow looms as the dirigible enters frame from above. The onlookers and people behind windows flee.

(S.E.) KRRRSH

The dirigible crash-lands and collapses under its own weight.

(S.E.) KRAK KRAK

As the dirigible collapses, it is caught between the tower and building.

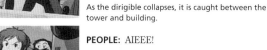

PEOPLE: AIEEE!

People panic, either running, frozen, or transfixed.

Broadcast Location

TV REPORTER: It's snagged on the building across the street where it's…

An onlooker from behind finds something as he shouts while looking at the dirigible tail. The reporter looks over too, amazed.
The camera shifts, too.

ONLOOKER: Hey, look! Over there!

Tiny Tombo is hanging from the rope, struggling to keep his grip.

TV REPORTER: It's a miracle! The young boy has somehow managed to keep his hold on the rope!

Tombo is desperately clinging onto the rope. The dirigible is crumbling apart.

TV REPORTER: But how can anyone rescue him now? That brave young boy is hanging on for dear life! He can't…

The reporter frantically shouts on the rooftop. Kiki flies up and passes over them.
He notices her.

TV REPORTER: Something just flew by!

Kiki flying toward Tombo. She zigzags and slows down, too.

TV REPORTER: (O.O.F.) It's a bird? No, it's not a bird. It's a young girl. No! It's a young witch soaring through the sky, and she's riding.

Old Lady's Mansion

Kiki winds around on the TV screen.
The lady and maid lean forward in excitement.

OLD LADY: Go, Kiki!
BARSA: Oh, my!

Bakery

Bakery kitchen.
Osono shouts from her couch.

OSONO: She can fly again!

Husband is amazed.

House on Cliff

The family with the stuffed animal watch TV. The dog is sleeping.

KET: Get 'im, Kiki!

In the Air

KIKI: Tombo!

Tombo barely dangling.
Kiki approaches him. He sees her.

TOMBO: Kiki!

Kiki reaches out. But the broom won't move properly. Kiki passes by.

KIKI: Oh! Tombo!

Tombo reaches out and slips.

TOMBO: Oh!

He grabs onto the end of the rope. Kiki flies O.O.F. Kiki drifts off.

KIKI: Come on now! Be a good broom!

She frantically takes charge of the brush, stops in the air and returns leaning over.
Kiki approaches Tombo. The crew in the gondola cheer her on.

CREW, CAPTAIN: Hang in there, my good lad!

Tombo reaches out, but the brush is incredibly unstable. It drops right before him, then it jerks upward. He's out of reach.

Kiki frantically reaches out, but she's swaying as if tossing about on rocky waves.

KIKI: Tombo!!
TOMBO: Kiki!

Tombo reaches out. He reaches out as far as he can.

Kiki approaches, Tombo reaches, and their hands touch.
All of a sudden the brush drops. Then it leaps up. It's unruly.

Broadcast Location

The reporter continues the live report. An onlooker cheers her on.

TV REPORTER: You can do it! Yes!
MAN: Don't give up now, sonny!

Park

Everyone cheers.
The three girls are there. The policeman's there too. Everyone including the firemen, cooks, and gentlemen shout.

EVERYONE: Don't give up!
Don't give up!
Don't give up!

The keeper in the clock tower also shouts.

KEEPER: Don't give up!

In the Air

Hands reaching out. Their fingers touch several times. They can't get any nearer. The cheering reaches them.

TOMBO: Urgh…

He's reaching out, but he can't hold on anymore. CLOSE on Tombo's hand. It trembles, then slips and grabs the rope. But he slips again and falls down O.O.F.

Central Park

Tombo falls toward the ground where the fire truck is parked with its red lights flashing.
Kiki also enters frame falling headfirst. The three girls and the policeman all scream.

City hall. Tombo and Kiki plummet through. The brush is suddenly suspended like a parachute opening up and slows down.

P.O.V. from below, slight upward angle. The reporter shouts.

TV REPORTER: She got him! She saved the youngster! I've never seen anything so amazing!

Everyone rushes forward. They're cheering.

CROWD: HURRAH

Everyone including the firefighters with their rescue net, the policemen, civilians, Tombo's friends rush forward.

Kiki and Tombo slowly descend. Everyone waits below. Some are waving from the city hall window.
Kiki and Tombo now fill up the frame above the cheering crowd. Tombo slowly lands on the rescue net.

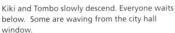

Kiki holds his hand.
Everyone welcomes them.
They cheer while others ring bells from their windows. People wave and toss out confetti.

TV REPORTER: Now she's bringing him down to land, safe and sound. She actually caught the boy in midair! And you saw it all live as she saved his life.

The crew wave from the gondola.

Street

The janitor is boasting to the crowd in front of the appliance store TV.

JANITOR: That broom she used was mine. That was my broom, you know!

Mansion

Barsa cheerfully spins the lady's chair.

OLD LADY: Oh, Barsa! Oh, my!
BARSA: Yippee!

Bakery

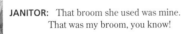

Osono teary-eyed.

OSONO: What a girl! Kiki was so brave. She really saved the day.

She realizes something. Pressing on her stomach, she addresses her husband.

OSONO: Uh-oh! Uh, better call the hospital, honey!
HUSBAND: Oh? Oh?
OSONO: I think it's time now!
HUSBAND: Oh! Oh, my!

Husband panics. He runs out, trips over a chair, and crashes.

(S.E.) TUMP TUMP KLAK KRRSSH

Central Park

Jiji weaves his way through the crowd.

Cameras everywhere. Kiki amazed by the flood of camera flashes.
Jiji skips into the frame, leaps onto her shoulder and meows over her shoulder.

KIKI: Jiji!
JIJI: Meow–

Of course, his voice will never return. But it doesn't matter anymore…
Kiki smiles and rubs her cheek against his.

Her Hometown

Her home, Kokiri. Okino just got her letter from the postman. He turns around and rushes home O.O.F.

Sunroom

Kokiri preparing a potion for Dora. Okino looks in the way Kiki did and shouts. Dora turns around.

OKINO: Hey! Listen, we just got a letter from Kiki.

Kokiri turns around, excited. When…

(S.E.) POOF

Once again, her potion ignites with a black puff of smoke.

OKINO: "Dear Mother and Father,
How are you doing? I'm happy to say that Jiji and I are doing fine at the moment."

Okino reading Kiki's letter. Kokiri leans in with her hand on his shoulder. Dora is smiling. CLOSE on horizontal writing of the letter.

KIKI: (O.O.F.) My delivery service is a big success. I've really started to gain some confidence…and everything is falling into place.

City Sky

City sky. Kiki flying gracefully.

KIKI: (O.O.F.) There are still some times when I feel a little homesick. But all in all, I sure love this city. I miss you. Lots of love, Kiki.

Kiki glides downward.
She's riding the deck brush with Jiji and the radio.
FADE OUT as her image shrinks off into the distance.

THE END

Tokuma Shoten, Yamato Transport and Nippon Television PRESENT
© 1989 Eiko Kadono - Nibariki - GN

OPENING CREDITS

EXECUTIVE PRODUCERS
Yasuyoshi Tokuma
Mikihiko Tsuzuki
Morihisa Takagi

ASSOCIATE EXECUTIVE PRODUCERS
Tatsumi Yamashita
Hideo Ogata
Iwai Seto

ORIGINAL STORY
Eiko Kadono (Published by Fukuinkan
Shoten Publishers)

SUPERVISING ANIMATORS
Shinji Otsuka
Katsuya Kondo
Yoshifumi Kondo

ART DIRECTION
Hiroshi Ono

CHARACTER DESIGN
Katsuya Kondo

MUSIC
Joe Hisaishi

COLOR DESIGN
Michiyo Yasuda

CAMERA SUPERVISOR
Juro Sugimura

EDITING
Takeshi Seyama

AUDIO DIRECTOR
Naoko Asari

RECORDING AND SOUND MIXING
Shuji Inoue

SOUND EFFECTS
Kazutoshi Sato

PRODUCTION
Toru Hara

ASSOCIATE PRODUCER
Toshio Suzuki

PRODUCED, WRITTEN & DIRECTED BY
Hayao Miyazaki

END CREDITS

VOICES

Minami Takayama	Hiroko Seki
Rei Sakuma	Koichi Miura
Mieko Nobuzawa	
Keiko Toda	Haruko Kato
Yamaguchi Kappei	

Masa Saito	Hiroko Maruyama
Chika Sakamoto	Yuko Tsuga
Mika Doi	Yoshiko Kamei
Yuko Kobayashi	Keiko Kagimoto
Yoshiko Asai	Yuriko Fuchizaki
Kikuko Inoue	Takaya Haji

Tomomichi Nishimura	Takashi Taguchi
Koichi Yamadera	Shinpachi Tsuji
Akio Otsuka	Michihiro Ikemizu
Brady Russell	Sharone Amann
Ken Larson	Ezaki Production

MUSIC DIRECTION
Isao Takahata

THEME SONGS
"Rouge no Dengon"
"Yasashisa ni Tsutsumaretanara"

PERFORMED BY
Yumi Arai (Alfa Records)

SOUNDTRACK ALBUM
Tokuma Japan

KEY ANIMATION

Yoshinori Kanada	Makiko Futaki
Masako Shinohara	Masaaki Endo
Toshio Kawaguchi	Atsuko Otani
Megumi Kagawa	Atsuko Fukushima

Toshiyuki Inoue	Noriko Moritomo
Koji Morimoto	Yoshiharu Sato
Natsuyo Yasuda	Sachiko Sugino
Hiroshi Watanabe	Hiroomi Yamakawa

Yukiyoshi Hane	Chie Uratani
Masahiro Sekino	Toshiya Niidome
Akiko Hasegawa	

ANIMATION CHECK

Yasuko Tachiki	Hitomi Tateno

INBETWEEN / CLEAN-UP ANIMATION

Ritsuko Shiina	Kazutaka Ozaki
Akiko Teshima	Takao Maki
Riwako Matsui	Kumiko Otani
Keiko Watanabe	Eiichiro Hirata
Naoko Takenawa	Akiko Yamaguchi
Nobuko Sato	Shiro Shibata
Nobuhiro Hosoi	Kazumi Okabe
Aki Yamagata	Hiroyuki Morita
Seiko Azuma	Keiko Nagai
Hitoshi Kagiyama	Ako Takano

Sumie Nishido / Rie Fujimura
Kiyoko Makita / Emiko Iwayanagi
Yutaka Ito / Makoto Suzuki
Masako Sakano / Hiroko Tetsuka
Akiko Matsushima / Yuka Endo
Katsumi Hiroe / Takuya Iinuma
Yurie Sudo / Machiko Araya
Mayumi Omura / Makoto Koga
Tatsuji Narita / Hiroyuki Kanbe
Nagisa Miyazaki / Tazuko Fukudo
Yumi Kawachi / Yuko Aoyama
Toshihiro Hamamori / Hideaki Maniwa
Setsuya Tanabe / Akihiko Nomura
Yoshie Hayashi / Koichi Taguchi
Yukari Yamaura / Katsusuke Konuma
Akiko Ishii / Tadaharu Takahashi
Koji Ito / Akio Watanabe
Hiroki Ikehata / Kasumi Hara
Akihiro Yuki / Yoshie Kawahashi
Yuriko Saito / Yoshimi Kanbara
Akihiko Adachi / Masayuki Shibuya
Etsuko Ishiwari / Reiko Mano
Ichiro Itsuki / Keiichi Suwada

SUPPORTING ANIMATION STUDIOS
Doga Kobo / Oh Production
Studio Hibari / Anime Torotoro
Studio Muku / Nakamura Production

BACKGROUND
Kazuo Oga / Satoshi Kuroda
Kazuhiro Kinoshita / Kiyomi Ota
Kyoko Naganawa / Yoko Nagashima

Kazuo Ebisawa / Yutaka Ito
Kiyoko Sugano / Hidetoshi Kaneko
Midori Chiba / Takashi Tokushige
Yuko Matsuura / Yuji Ikehata
Studio Fuga
Toshiharu Mizutani / Kenji Kamiyama
Miyuki Kudo / Kumiko Ono

SPECIAL EFFECTS
Kaoru Tanifuji

HARMONY TREATMENT
Noriko Takaya

FEATURED ARTWORK
"Niji no Ue wo Tobu Fune"
Painted by the students of Hachinohe City
Minato Special Junior High School for the
Handicapped

STILL PHOTO
Junichi Ochiai

KIKI LOGO DESIGN
Akiko Hayashi

INK AND PAINT CHECK
Yumi Furuya / Noriko Ogawa
Teruyo Tateyama / Yuki Hisada
Ikuyo Kimura

COLOR DESIGN ASSISTANT
Yuriko Katayama

INK AND PAINT
IM Studio
Michiyo Iseda / Reiko Aonuma
Michiko Shibata / Hideko Sato
Eiko Fukuma / Yoko Tanida
Mariko Konuma / Rumi Fukaya
Eiko Horikiri / Mieko Nakano
Kazue Hiranuma / Yukari Tajima

Studio Killy
Toshichika Iwakiri / Naomi Takahashi
Nobuko Watanabe / Tatsuko Kubota
Harumi Machii / Toshiko Tawara
Mayumi Watabe / Mieko Asai
Yuriko Kudo / Miyoko Oka
Kazumi Kobayashi / Ritsuko Osaki

Trace Studio M
Fumiko Ito / Mika Tanifuji
Taeko Omi / Tsutomu Muta
Michiko Nishimaki / Masami Nishizaka
Yukari Yokoyama / Izumi Maeno

Dragon Production
Reiko Yoshida / Midori Sugawara

Domusha
Chieko Omachi / Masuko Suganuma
Studio OZ / Studio Fantasia
Yukimi Toyonaga / Toy House
Junko Yoshikawa / Kyoto Animation

CAMERA
Studio Gallop
Yasuhiro Shimizu / Katsuya Kozutsumi
Hisao Kazemura / Kenji Akazawa
Toru Kobayashi / Yasunori Hayama
Josaku Nishiyama / Tomoshi Arakawa
Hiroaki Edamitsu / Hiroshi Tamura

ASSISTANT TO THE DIRECTOR
Sunao Katabuchi

PRODUCTION MANAGER
Eiko Tanaka

PRODUCTION DESK
Toshiyuki Kawabata / Hirokatsu Kihara

PRODUCTION ASSISTANTS
Toshitaka Henmi / Tomoaki Nishigiri
Yuji Kitazawa / Hiroyuki Ito

SOUND EFFECTS ASSISTANTS
Hironori Ono / Norio Kobayashi

RECORDING STUDIO
Tokyo T.V. Center

EDITING ASSISTANT
Hiroshi Adachi

RECORDING PRODUCTION
Omnibus Promotion

DIALOG EDITING
Fujio Yamada

RECORDING SUPPORT
Shoichi Tamaasa

FILM DEVELOPING
Telescreen
Toei Chemical Industry

PRODUCTION SUPPORT
Animage Editorial Department
Group Fudosha

PRODUCTION COORDINATOR
Yoko Umemura

ADVERTISING PRODUCER
Masaya Tokuyama

PUBLICITY SUPPORT
Dentsu

TITLES
Kaoru Mano
Akira Michikawa

TECHNICAL COOPERATION
Taiyo Shikisai Stac

Technical Cooperation
Continental Far East Inc
Mikio Mori

"Majyo no Takkyubin"
PRODUCTION COMMITTEE
Tokuma Shoten
Hiroyuki Kato / Akira Kaneko
Atsushi Miura / Michio Yokoo
Yoshio Tsuboike
Yamato Transport
Akiji Ota / Hiroshi Tojo
Yoshifumi Kitanokuchi
Nippon Television Network
Seiji Urushido / Takeo Mutai
Muneyoshi Yokoyama / Seiji Okuda

PRODUCTION
Studio Ghibli

Owari (The End)

THE ART OF

KIKI's
DELIVERY SERVICE

BASED ON A STUDIO GHIBLI FILM

FROM THE NOVEL BY EIKO KADONO
SCREENPLAY WRITTEN, DIRECTED AND PRODUCED BY HAYAO MIYAZAKI

Original Edition Edited by Studio Ghibli

English Adaptation/Yuji Oniki
Design & Layout/Hidemi Sahara
Editor/Eric Searleman

Majo no Takkyubin (Kiki's Delivery Service)
© 1989 Eiko Kadono - Studio Ghibli - N
All drawings and storyboards © 1989 Studio Ghibli - N
All rights reserved.
First published in Japan by Tokuma Shoten Co., Ltd.

This book was originally published in Japan in 1989. The creators' profiles and
other contents of the book are current for that publication date only.

Printed in Korea

Published by VIZ Media, LLC
P.O. Box 77010
San Francisco, CA 94107

First printing, May 2006
Ninth printing, April 2022

Visit www.viz.com